MISSOURI
Welcomes You

WELCOME TO
MISSOURI
U.S.A.

Missouri
BACK ROAD RESTAURANT
Recipes

A Cookbook & Restaurant Guide

ANITA MUSGROVE

Great American Publishers
www.GreatAmericanPublishers.com

TOLL-FREE 1-888-854-5954

Great American Publishers

501 Avalon Way Suite B • Brandon, MS 39047
TOLL-FREE 1-888-854-5954 • www.GreatAmericanPublishers.com

ISBN 978-1-934817-28-5

by Anita Musgrove

First Edition

10 9 8 7 6 5 4 3 2 1

Front cover: toasted ravioli, bhofack2 • road, jwdorris • sign, Diane Diederich • Page 1: Missouri sign, fotoguy22 • cavern, Brian Wathen • Page 2: Welcome to Missouri sign, roxanabalint • baseball & glove, miflippo • ball of twine, David Commins • Pony Express Stamp, Kenneth Wiedemann • miniature Missouri flags, Bosphorus • Donkey, Coprid • Route 66 sign, kojihirano • Page 3: State of Missouri stamp, SunChan • Page 5:fiddle, Cesare Andrea Ferrari • iced tea, Paul Johnson • food plate, Cook's Corner Café • Page 6: rib plate, BB's Lawnside BBQ • Page 7: guest check, DNY59 • toy train, kyoshino • car key, andegro4ka • sunglasses, uric • Page 8: sign, mum_ble • Page 9: red paper cup, vitalssss • Page 10: Walt Disney Stamp, traveler1116 • slice of bread, joebelanger • pecan halves, gerenme • Page 11: steam boat toy, &#169 Rod MacPherson • plastic building blocks, Jordan McCullough • pile of pancakes, NatalyaAksenova • green barrel, unclepodger • green wooden toy car, ThomasVogel • baseball, bat & glove, eurobanks • Page 47: Wine cellar, Arabia Steamboat Museum • paddle wheel, Arabia Steamboat Museum • Page 62-63: cup & saucer, ZinaidaSopina • Tom Sawyer stamp, traveler1116 • ice cream cone, Madllen • wallet, LucianoBibulichPage • parachute, ZargonDesign • hot dog, Rpsycho • tickets, chess piece, cscredon adempercem • pick axe, ikanchan999 • Page 72-73: All images, www.HannibalHistoryMuseum. com • Page 93: Jesse James Hideout, By Superphoebe a.k.a. Phoebe Owens via Wikimedia Commons • Page 98: Pizza, Proformabooks • Page 99: Cheeseburger and fries, rez-art • chicken wings, mphillips007 • Page 104-105: Museum images, www.citymuseum.org • Page 116: Shopping cart,YinYang • Page 117: coffee cup, posteriori • Missouri State Flag, MicroStockHub • bluebird, WMarissen • turtle with suitcase, Anton. Sokolov • garden gnome, Valerie Loiseleux • ketchup bottle, Richard Tas • salt & pepper shakers, 4nadia • wallet, LucianoBibulichPage • red telephone receiver,BrianAJackson Page 121-121: Clydesdales/WarmSprings Ranch, www.warmspringsranch.com • Page 130-131: Missouri State Penitentiary images, www.missouripentours.com • Page 138-139: All images, Cindy Brenneke -Where Pigs Fly Farm • Page 156-157: sunglasses, urric • coin, maogg • rock, Melissa Carroll • knife and fork in a napkin, plimages • Cup, vitalssss • cookie jar, EllenMol1814 • tornado, Ivcandy • banjo, tomazl • bullets, NorthStar203 • hard hat, ikanchan999 • Page 168-169: Rutledge-Wilson images, Springfield-Greene County Park Board • Page 178-179: all images, Will Tollerton/Bushwacker Museum • Page 186-187: all images, Fantastic Caverns • Page 188-189: cupcake, juliannafunk • sunglasses, keys, & map, DNY59 • travel Cup, AdShooter • camera, pakornkrit • flying bee, Antagain • rocking chair, pterwort • whitethorn flower, scisettialfio • guest check, DNY59 • buttons, phive2015 • Page 196-197: All images, www.bonneterremine.com • Page 204-205: crawfish, sixty7a • cartoon crawfish, daveturton • crawfish etouffee, sf_foodphoto • snow crab legs, mphillips007 • oysters, James the Food Photographer • Page 214-215: All images, www.cavevineyard.com • Page 220-221: All Images, The Vacuum Museum • Page 228: baseball, glove, & bat, eurobanks • Page 236: suitcase, Rouzes • car key and sunglasses on roadmap, DNY59 • Back Cover: barbeque nachos, Smith Creek Moonshine • wallet, LucianoBilbulich • ball of twine, David Commins • whitethorn flower, scisettialfio • plastic building blocks, Jordan McCullough • chess piece, cscredon adempercem • coffee cup, posteriori • car key, andegro4ka

Every effort has been made to ensure the accuracy of the information provided in this book.
However, dates, times, and locations are subject to change.
Please call or visit websites for up-to-date information before traveling.

To purchase books in quantity for corporate use, incentives, or fundraising,
please call Great American Publishers at 888-854-5954.

Contents

Preface

Hey, it's just me again, cranking up the old Mercury to go on another road trip. This time I'm bringing you the best locally owned places to eat and enjoy in Missouri. This has become quite an adventure to be able to go from state to state to learn about each unique Mom and Pop restaurant. We have already been to Alabama, Kentucky, Tennessee and Texas and now the journey continues with a trip across Missouri. My hope is that you enjoy the STATE BACK ROAD RESTAURANT SERIES as much as I have enjoyed bringing it to you. Just toss the book in the car and we'll explore the five regions together.

We'll start in the Northwest Region where you will find **Rolling Pin Bakery** in Glasgow. There is nothing like a good warm cinnamon roll with a cold glass of chocolate milk first thing in the morning. (Yes, I prefer milk over coffee; that is just the kid in me.) Try the *Iced Snickerdoodles* (page 29) while you are there. You may even run into the "ladies" there. Read about them in the book—it's quite a story. Bring your cooler

and stop at **Kurzweil's Country Meats** where you can take home "Raised on the Farm" meats. Or, eat in and get them to serve you *Smoked Pork Chops with Apple Glaze* (page 27). In all, you will find 22 outstanding, locally-owned restaurants in the Northwestern region.

THWESTERN
REGION

NORTHEASTERN
REGION

CENTRAL
REGION

SOUTHWESTERN
REGION

SOUTHEASTERN
REGION

Next, we'll cut across to the Northeast Region where you will find Marshall (pronounced Mar-shell) at the **South 63 Café** in Macon. This lady runs the café like she does her home—you are always welcome and she feeds not only your stomach, but also your soul. She will tell you to come and join the other nuts in the café and enjoy yourself with laughter, teasing, wisdom and a blessing to take you on your way. If you leave hungry, it will be your own fault. The portions are big at a reasonable price and you will get a "Bless You" when you waddle out the door. Try the recipe for *Coconut Cream Pie* (page 85), my father's favorite, or the *Hand-Breaded Tenderloin* (page 84).

Later, we'll visit **Mama Campisi's On the Hill** in St. Louis where you will learn the fascinating story about when Fried Ravioli was first created. There are 22 restaurants in this region, also, and I can tell you, each restaurant is as good as the one before.

Now let's jump to the Central Region right in the middle of Missouri. Tired yet? Stop at the **Iron Horse Hotel and Restaurant**, get some rest and enjoy the *Bananas Foster Cheesecake* (page 119). YUM. Enjoy a walk through the past reflecting on the glory days of the railroad barons in their furnishings; if Tracy is there, he'll tell you the stories. Don't forget to stop in **Sweetwater BBQ** in Saint Robert. Say hello to Ms. Saxton for me and enjoy barbecue done right. Don't forget to try some of *Judy's Everything Carrot Cake* (page 147). Too full to eat there? Go home and make it yourself with her recipe. You will find 15 locally owned places featured in this region.

Let's drop down to the Southeast Region, as we continue our journey and visit Toni Brown at the **Fiddler's Fish House** in Dexter. Toni learned this business from the pond up, you may say. She serves great fish—from pond to plate—along with sides including her *Vinegar Slaw* (page 201). Her daughter Layla works by her side; Fiddler's is truly a family run business. Drop in and visit **Strawberry's BBQ** as you pass through Holcomb. Enjoy his beans, slaw and legendary 2-pound pork steak—it really is as big as a dinner plate. I hope you will have time to visit all 14 restaurants included in this region.

Okay let's finish our tour with the Southwest Region and we will have come full circle through Missouri. **Uncle Rooster's** in Seymour, with the big white rooster prominently displayed out front, is sure to grab your attention. Come in and visit with Wayne "Rooster" Durning, check out the locally made crafts for sale and even sign your name on the floor so everyone will know you have been there. Have I told you that a good hot dog is my favorite comfort food? Uncle Rooster's serves the best Chicago dog; it will give you something to crow about. As you travel to Branson and turn a curve in the road at the base of the, what I call a mountain—I was informed it was just a really tall hill, you will come across **Dana's Bar B Que and Burger Shop**. The smell of barbecue smoking will reach you long before you find Dana's, they are well known for the best old-fashioned hickory smoked barbecue around. They smoke their meats 12 to 14 hours every night over hickory wood so the smell is incredible. These two restaurants along with 10 more will keep you well-fed when traveling in this region.

After losing Leonard to cancer back in 2011, I had to find another road buddy. My Grandson Nic traveled with me for a while, but now that he has turned 18, he has other things on his mind —girls, work, hunting, hanging with the guys. Granny isn't top priority in his world now, so I had to find another traveling friend. God has blessed me with Richard Shaw. I wonder how long it will take him to get tired of being "lost" for hours? As we travel along, Richard and I wonder at the things we see like the steeple still pointing toward heaven while the walls around it have gone. What happened to the old church? What about the old chimney standing in the middle of a field? I'm thankful that he's by my side on my road trips these days.

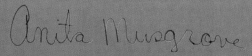

Of course, even with new travel partners, one thing never changes. Wherever our travels take us, we always search out the locally owned restaurants for a great meal. I suggest you get in your car and travel, too. Just go right and see where it will lead you. When you get hungry, you may be surprised at Mom and Pop places near where you are. Travel near a river or large stream, and I bet you will find a great catfish place to eat. I have. Sniff the air, smell that hickory wood burning, bet it is a barbecue place or a steak dive. I hope you will get out, enjoy life, and experience things you do not normally get to enjoy ... and support the locally owned places to eat while you are there. Where's the keys? Let's go!

Anita Musgrove

Northwestern REGION

Pin Oak Hill Restaurant

Pin Oak Hill Game Management Area, Inc.
13396 Z Highway
Bogard, MO 64622
660-745-3030
www.facebook.com/PinOakHill

Pin Oak Hill Restaurant, set in the picturesque rolling hills and crop land of northwest Missouri, is renowned for excellent prime rib and a wide range of certified Angus beef steaks. Other entréess include smothered chicken, salmon, and pork chops. Chef Jerry makes all the desserts and one of his specialties is cheesecake. The red velvet cheesecake is a house favorite and one that customers really enjoy. Condiments are all made in house and available for purchase in the restaurant. Whatever you decide, relax and settle into the Missouri countryside for an amazing meal, and enjoy a drink from the bar.

Wednesday & Thursday: 5:00 pm to 9:00 pm
Friday & Saturday: 4:00 pm to 10:00 pm
Saturday & Sunday: 11:00 am to 2:00 pm

Creamy Parmesan Dressing

1½ cups mayonnaise

½ cup sour cream

1½ tablespoons granulated onion

1 tablespoon granulated garlic

1 cup white wine

1 tablespoon pepper

1½ cups grated Parmesan

Mix ingredients in a large bowl; chill. Serve over your favorite mixed greens. Will make approximately 1 pint. Store in refrigerator for up to 2 weeks.

Family Favorite

Tomato Florentine

5 tablespoons butter, divided

3 tablespoons flour

2 tablespoons olive oil

1 medium onion, diced

1 tablespoon minced fresh garlic

1 cup chicken stock

1 (28-ounce) can crushed tomatoes

¾ cup V8 juice

1 tablespoon chopped fresh basil
or 2 teaspoons dried basil

1 tablespoon dried dill

1 teaspoon sugar

2 teaspoons salt

1 teaspoon pepper

1 tablespoon red wine (optional)

2 cups heavy cream

½ cup chopped spinach

In a skillet, heat 3 tablespoons butter and flour over medium heat until fully incorporated; set aside. In large pot over medium heat, sauté 2 tablespoons butter, olive oil, onion and garlic; simmer 5 minutes. Add chicken stock, crushed tomatoes, V8, basil, dill, sugar, salt, pepper and wine; simmer 15 minutes. Whisk in flour mixture; simmer 20 minutes. Add heavy cream and spinach; cook another 5 minutes. Serve.

Family Favorite

Boji Stone Café

612 Washington Street
Chillicothe, MO 64601
660-646-9939
bojistonecafé.com
facebook.com/bojistonecafé

Boji Stone Café, Coffee House & Bookstore has been giving the folks of Chillicothe something to talk about since 2006, offering a slightly different slant on the typical local menu standards. They have a "Better Be Ho'made" attitude. From salad dressings, soups, pasta sauces, and even croutons to the cheesecake and ice cream...it is all made from scratch daily, with love and family pride. In addition to amazing food and unique books, there is an assortment of Coffee House Favorites...steaming hot lattes and cappuccinos, frozen frappes, and fruit smoothies. Boji Stone Café is located on the square in beautiful downtown Chillicothe.

Monday–Wednesday, Friday & Saturday: 7:00 am to 5:00 pm
Thursday: 7:00 am to 8:00pm
Sunday: 9:00 am to 3:00 pm

Blue Cheese Dressing

1½ cups mayonnaise
1 cup buttermilk
1 teaspoon sugar
½ teaspoon black pepper
2 teaspoons grated garlic
¼ teaspoon onion powder
¼ teaspoon salt
1 cup blue cheese crumbles

Using an electric mixer, combine mayonnaise, buttermilk, sugar, pepper, garlic, onion powder and salt. Fold in blue cheese. Refrigerate 12 hours before use.

Restaurant Recipe

Banana Muffins

3 cups sugar

1⅓ cups shortening

4 eggs, beaten

½ cup sour cream

8 smashed super-ripe bananas

4 cups all-purpose flour

2 tablespoons baking soda

¼ teaspoon salt

2 teaspoons vanilla bean paste

1 cup chopped nuts, if you
are feeling nutty

In a large bowl using an electric mixer, cream sugar and shortening until light and fluffy. Using a fork, add remaining ingredients, mixing lightly until just combined. Place in lined jumbo muffin cups. Bake at 350° for 25 to 30 minutes.

Great Grandmas Weber's Recipe

Chillicoffee Toffee Ice Cream

1 large egg

5 large egg yolks

1½ cups sugar

¼ cup unsweetened cocoa powder

½ cup freeze-dried coffee

4 cups heavy whipping cream

2 cups milk

5 frozen toffee bars, smashed

In a metal bowl using a wire whisk, beat egg and egg yolks for 5 minutes until light, fluffy and pale yellow. Slowly add sugar while beating; continue to beat 1 additional minute. Add cocoa and coffee, mixing until dissolved. Whisk in cream and milk; whisking vigorously for 1 additional minute. Refrigerate until temperature reaches 45 degrees. Pour into electric freezer; freeze according to manufacturer's directions. Just before completely frozen, add toffee bars.

Restaurant Recipe

PC's Elkhorn Steakhouse

609 Jackson Street
Chillicothe, MO 64601
660-646-2804
www.pcselkhornsteakhouse.com

The downtown historical area of Chillicothe is known as a city of murals and home of sliced bread. PC's Elkhorn Steakhouse, located one block east of the square in a historical building from 1925, has been offering guests home cooking, like grandma used to make, in a rustic old-time setting since 2001. Enjoy Connie's down-home goodness in a rustic setting of a blend of country, game hunting, and the Old West. Enjoy home cooking, real mashed potatoes, hand-cut and breaded tenderloins, and top-of-the-line choice steaks grilled the way you order them. See you all there soon.

Monday & Tuesday: 6:00 am to 2:00 pm
Wednesday & Thursday: 6:00 am to 8:00 pm
Friday & Saturday: 6:00 am to 9:00 pm

Punch Bowl Cake

1 box yellow cake mix, plus ingredients to cook

2 (4.6-ounce) boxes cook-and-serve vanilla pudding, plus ingredients to cook

3 large bananas

1 (20-ounce) can crushed pineapple, do not drain

1 (16-ounce) carton Cool Whip

1 (16-ounce) bag frozen strawberries, sweetened

Nuts for topping

Bake cake in 2 round cake pans; cool. Cook pudding according to package directions; cool in refrigerator. In the bottom of a large punch bowl, place 1 layer of cake; poke holes in layer with fork. Slice 2 bananas on top of cake; pour pineapple with juice over bananas. Spread half the pudding on top of pineapple; top with thin layer of Cool Whip. Add second cake layer; poke holes in cake with fork. Slice remaining banana on top of cake; add frozen strawberries. Layer with remaining pudding. Finish with Cool Whip on top; garnish with nuts.

Family Favorite

Decadent Brownie Pie

1 (9-inch) unbaked pastry shell

1 cup semisweet chocolate chips

¼ cup butter or margarine

1 (14-ounce) can Eagle Brand creamy chocolate-flavored condensed milk

½ cup biscuit baking mix

2 eggs, beaten

1 teaspoon vanilla extract

1 cup chopped nuts

Vanilla ice cream

Preheat oven to 375°. Bake pastry shell 10 minutes; remove from oven. Reduce heat to 325°. In a saucepan over low heat, melt chips with margarine. In a mixer bowl, beat chocolate mixture with Eagle Brand, biscuit mix, eggs and vanilla until smooth. Add nuts; pour into pastry shell. Bake 35 to 40 minutes or until center is set. Serve warm with ice cream.

Family Favorite

GREATEST THING SINCE SLICED BREAD
Home of Sliced Bread, Chillicothe

Chillicothe Baking Company first introduced the world to sliced bread on July 6, 1928. In an advertisement from around that time, owner Frank Bench boasted about his Kleen Maid Sliced Bread. Saying, "Just think of it! Every slice perfect and CORRECT, far better than you could cut it yourself. There was a time when you ground coffee. Now you buy it ground. Well, this is the same sort of sensible, logical improvement."

The sliced bread sold by Chillicothe Baking Company was also advertised as "the greatest forward step in the baking industry since bread was wrapped." This led to the popular phrase, "greatest thing since sliced bread."

We take it for granted today, but there was a time that "sliced bread"—a loaf of bread that has been sliced with a machine and packaged for convenience—was unheard of by busy moms of the day. Since the beginning of civilization, bread was made in loaves that had to be cut to size by hand. Previous efforts to mechanize the process resulted in squashed slices of bread.

Then along came Otto Rohwedder of Davenport, Iowa. His did the job with multiple knives that sliced from the top and the bottom at the same time. Two metal pins inserted at each end held the loaf together while it was wrapped in paper. When the housewife was ready to use the bread, the wrapper was opened and one pin taken out. Enough slices for the meal were removed and the wrapper was folded closed.

However, it was almost NOT the greatest thing since sliced bread, because nobody wanted Rohwedder's machine. He had worked on the device for more than a decade, but bakers were skeptical, fearing the bread would go stale. When Bench decided to give the machine a try, his Kleen Maid Bread quickly became very popular, increasing their sales by 2,000 percent in just a few weeks.

The city of Chillicothe decided to honor this monumental event and in 2007 made their official town slogan: "The Home of Sliced Bread."

City of Chillicothe
888-756-0990
www.chillicothecity.org

FUN FACTS:

- U.S. officials banned sliced bread on January 18, 1943, as a conservation effort during the war. The ban was very unpopular with housewives of the day and lasted less than three months.

- Rohwedder sold his three jewelry stores to fund the development effort and to manufacture his bread-slicing machines.

- In 1917, a fire broke out at the factory where Rohwedder was manufacturing his machine. It destroyed his prototype and blueprints.

- In 1927, Rohwedder obtained a patent on an improved machine that not only sliced the bread, but wrapped it.

- By coincidence Frank Bench went into production with the machine on Rohwedder's 48th birthday.

- The first loaf of sliced bread was sold commercially on July 7, 1928, at Chillicothe Baking Company, owned by Frank Bench.

a marker at the original site of the bakery

Dempsey's BBQ

103 Northeast 2nd Street
Concordia, MO 64020
660-463-7232
www.dempseysbbq.com
www.facebook.com/DempseysBBQConcordiaMO

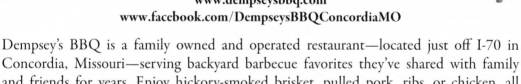

Dempsey's BBQ is a family owned and operated restaurant—located just off I-70 in Concordia, Missouri—serving backyard barbecue favorites they've shared with family and friends for years. Enjoy hickory-smoked brisket, pulled pork, ribs, or chicken, all made with homemade rubs and served with their signature bourbon barbecue sauce. Try the homemade baked beans, coleslaw, macaroni & cheese, green beans, broccoli & cheese, hand-cut fries, or smoked cream cheese. The rubs and bourbon barbecue sauce are created by Dempsey's, and are available for purchase when you stop in. Their beef is locally grown, 100% certified Hereford.

Sunday–Thursday: 11:00 am to 9:00 pm
Friday & Saturday: 11:00 am to 11:00 pm

Sausage Sauerkraut Balls

1 pound pork breakfast sausage

1 onion, finely chopped

1 teaspoon garlic powder

3 tablespoons plus 1 cup all-purpose flour, divided

2 cups sauerkraut, drained, chopped coarsely

4 ounces cream cheese, softened

1 teaspoon dry mustard

1 teaspoon black pepper, plus more for coating

4 large eggs, divided

3 cups breadcrumbs

Salt to taste

2 quarts vegetable oil

Line rimmed baking sheet with parchment paper. Cook sausage, onion and garlic powder in a nonstick skillet over medium heat, breaking sausage into small pieces with spoon, until no longer pink. Stir in 3 tablespoons flour until incorporated; remove from heat. Stir in sauerkraut, cream cheese, dry mustard and pepper until cream cheese melts. Let mixture cool for 10 minutes; stir in 1 beaten egg.

Divide mixture into 36 portions; roll into balls; place on baking sheet. Place remaining 1 cup flour in shallow dish; beat 3 eggs in second shallow dish. Place breadcrumbs seasoned with salt and pepper to taste in third shallow dish. Roll balls in flour, dip in eggs, then coat with breadcrumbs. Place balls on 2 large plates; freeze until firm, about 30 minutes. Heat oil, 1½ inches deep in skillet, to 350°. Fry until golden brown, 3 to 5 minutes.

Family Favorite

Ray's Diner

231 East Broadway Street
Excelsior Springs, MO 64024
816-637-3432
Find us on Facebook

Ray's Diner, the oldest diner in Clay County, was established in 1932, seating ten people. It moved across the street in 1942, but still uses the original ten barstools, original grill, cash register, original hamburger press, and the same chili recipe. Come and admire one of the biggest Pepsi collections ever created. They were picked as the December Restaurant in *Missouri Rural Magazine*. The customers love to read about and reminisce about the businesses from 1957, through articles that are preserved on the counter. Brenda says, "We look forward to you coming and seeing us."

Monday–Saturday: 6:00 am to 2:00 pm

Meatloaf

1 cup breadcrumbs

¼ cup milk

2 pounds hamburger

¾ cup chopped onion

½ cup chopped bell pepper

3 eggs, beaten

¼ cup oatmeal

1 (8-ounce) package shredded
pepper jack cheese

¼ cup ketchup

¼ cup barbecue sauce

2 tablespoons honey

2 tablespoons brown sugar

Preheat oven to 375°. In a bowl, soak breadcrumbs with milk; set aside. In another bowl, mix hamburger, onion, pepper, eggs, oatmeal and breadcrumbs; mix well. Place in a baking pan, forming a loaf. Make a trench down middle of loaf; push cheese in trench, pinching together to seal. In a bowl, combine ketchup, barbecue sauce, honey and brown sugar; mix well. Pour over meatloaf; bake 1 hour.

Restaurant Recipe
Customer Favorite

Homemade Chicken and Noodles

10 cups water

3 chicken breasts

2 teaspoons salt, divided

3 cups all-purpose flour, plus
extra for rolling dough

4 eggs, beaten

3 drops yellow food coloring

In a stockpot, bring water to a boil; add chicken and 1 teaspoon salt. Boil until chicken is done. Remove chicken from broth; set aside. In a bowl, place 1½ cups broth to cool down; you may have to add an ice cube to cool. In a separate bowl, add flour, 1 teaspoon salt and eggs; mix well while slowly adding cooled broth to form slightly sticky dough. Spread flour on flat surface; roll dough to ¼-inch thickness. Cut into strips with pizza cutter. Add strips to boiling broth. Add food coloring; turn heat to low. Simmer 20 minutes. Chop chicken; add to pot.

Restaurant Recipe

Ventana Gourmet Grill

117 West Broadway Street
Excelsior Springs, MO 64024
816-630-8600
www.tasteofmissouri.com/ventana

Ventana is located in the historical Hall of Waters District. The nostalgia is apparent as you walk into the restaurant with the original wood floors, tin ceilings, and brick walls. Ventana's menu is known for its pastas and steaks, but also serves seafood, burgers, sandwiches, and more. A great wine menu and full bar are also available. Don't pass up the homemade cheesecakes or bread pudding to end your exquisite meal.

Monday–Thursday: 11:00 am to 8:30 pm
Friday & Saturday: 11:00 am to 9:30 pm

Roasted Red Pepper Bruschetta

1 cup chopped roasted red peppers

1 medium red tomato, chopped

½ small red onion, chopped

Fresh basil-to taste, a good handful

1 or 2 cloves garlic, crushed

4 tablespoons olive oil

2 tablespoons balsamic vinegar

Salt and pepper to taste

1 baguette loaf, sliced

Combine all ingredients, except bread. Mix well. Serve on buttered and grilled baguette slices.

Restaurant Recipe

Ventana Bread Pudding

1 (20-ounce) can crushed pineapple

7 eggs, beaten

1 quart half-and-half (more if too dry)

2 teaspoons vanilla

1 cup sugar

½ teaspoon cinnamon (optional)

1 large loaf sourdough bread, thickly sliced and cubed

Preheat oven to 350°. Butter a 9x13-inch casserole dish; set aside. In a bowl, combine pineapple, eggs, half-and-half, vanilla, sugar and cinnamon. Fold in bread cubes; set aside 10 minutes to absorb liquid. Pour into prepared dish. Bake 30 to 40 minutes until golden brown.

Hazelnut Caramel Sauce:

½ stick butter

1½ cups brown sugar

¼ cup liquid hazelnut syrup

In a saucepan, melt butter; stir in brown sugar. Bring to a boil; cook 2 to 3 minutes. Add syrup; stir well. Pour over bread pudding before serving. Garnish with whipped cream and a dash of cinnamon.

Restaurant Recipe

Kurzweils' Country Meats

28612 South State Route T
Garden City, MO 64747
816-773-6547
www.kurzweilsmeats.com
Find us on Facebook

Since 1995, Kurzweils' Country Meats has been a family-owned business offering "Raised on the Farm" quality meats. All items are freshly prepared and made to order. Lunch is served daily from 11 to 3. Kurzweils' proudly makes a variety of smoked meat selections, including bacon, brisket, chicken, turkey, smoked bratwursts and sausages, whole smoked hams, fresh-cut steaks, and their famous smoked pork chops. They offer a great selection of spices, marinades, and local jams and jellies that provide a true taste of Missouri, as well as providing catering services, online ordering, and shipping.

Monday–Saturday: 9:00 am to 5:30 pm
Sunday: 11:00 am to 5:00 pm
Lunch served daily: 11:00 am to 3:00 pm

FAMILY OWNED
KURZWEILS
SINCE ★ 1995
MAKING GOOD MEALS GREAT!

One Pot Andouille Sausage Pasta Skillet

This incredibly cheesy pasta dish easily comes together in less than thirty minutes in one skillet—even the pasta gets cooked right in the pan.

1 tablespoon olive oil

2 cloves garlic, minced

1 onion, diced

1 (12.8-ounce) package smoked andouille sausage, thinly sliced

2 cups chicken broth

1 (14.5-ounce) can diced tomatoes

½ cup milk

8 ounces elbow pasta

Kosher salt and freshly ground black pepper to taste

1 cup shredded pepper jack cheese

Heat olive oil in a large skillet over medium-high heat; add garlic, onion and sausage. Cook, stirring frequently, until sausage is lightly browned. Stir in chicken broth, tomatoes, milk and pasta; season with salt and pepper. Bring to a boil; cover. Reduce heat; simmer until pasta is cooked through, 12 to 14 minutes. Remove from heat; top with cheese. Cover until cheese has melted.

Restaurant Recipe

Smoked Pork Chops with Apple Glaze

1 Kurzweils smoked pork chop per serving

1 container Kurzweils Apple Glaze

1 cup water

Preheat oven to 350°. Place pork chops in a single layer in an oven-safe dish; add water. Warm in oven 20 to 25 minutes; remove. Place a generous spoonful of apple glaze on each chop. Return to oven under broiler long enough for glaze to start browning. Ready to serve.

Restaurant Recipe

© Debbie Johnson

© Debbie Johnson

Rolling Pin Bakery

104 Market Street
Glasgow, MO 65254
660-338-0800
Find us on Facebook

The Rolling Pin Bakery is located in historic downtown Glasgow on the Missouri River. For breakfast, enjoy a variety of pastries, including cinnamon rolls, muffins, Danishes, and turnovers. Their lunch menu includes seasonal homemade soups and many delicious hot and cold sandwiches—Reubens, chicken wraps, and homemade chicken salad to name a few. For dessert, sample an assortment of made-from-scratch pies, cakes, cheesecakes, and cookies. Enjoy your meal next to picture glass windows, hardwood floors, and a pressed tin ceiling. Or you can choose to sit on the shady patio featuring a stunning bent copper waterfall wall.

Tuesday–Saturday: 7:00 am to 3:00 pm

Carrot Cake

2 cups grated carrots

10 ounces crushed pineapple

2 cups shredded coconut

3 eggs

1½ cups vegetable oil

2 cups sugar

2¼ cups all-purpose flour

1 teaspoon salt

2 teaspoons baking soda

2 teaspoons cinnamon

1 teaspoon vanilla

In a bowl, mix all ingredients with a wooden spoon. Pour into 3 greased and floured 9-inch pans, lined with wax paper. Bake at 375° for 30 minutes or until done. Ice with Cream Cheese Icing.

Cream Cheese Icing:

2 (8-ounce) packages cream cheese, softened

2 sticks margarine, softened

8 cups powdered sugar

Beat cream cheese and butter until smooth; add powdered sugar. Frost cake.

Restaurant Recipe

Iced Snickerdoodles

2 cups margarine

2 cups plus 2 teaspoons sugar, divided

2 (3.4-ounce) packages instant vanilla pudding

4 eggs

2 teaspoons baking soda

2 teaspoons cinnamon, divided

1 teaspoon salt

3 teaspoons vanilla, divided

5 cups all-purpose flour

3 cups powdered sugar

⅛ cup milk

In mixer, cream margarine, 2 cups sugar and pudding. Add eggs, baking soda, 1 teaspoon cinnamon, salt and 2 teaspoons vanilla; add flour. Make into balls; roll in mixture of 1 teaspoon cinnamon and 2 teaspoons sugar. Place on lined cookie sheet. Flatten with palms of hand. Bake at 350° for 5 minutes; rotate pan. Bake another 5 minutes. Mix powdered sugar, milk and 1 teaspoon vanilla to make glaze. Spread glaze over cookies.

Restaurant Recipe

Hank & Tank's BBQ

408 North Davis Street
Hamilton, MO 64644
816-649-8474

Tucked away in a former gas station, Hank and Tank's is a small-town, family-friendly, overall great place to taste some of the finest smoked meats in Missouri. Their pulled pork sandwiches and baked beans can't be beat. Don't forget the brisket, pork loin, coleslaw and turkey...if you are early enough to get it before it is sold out. Lowell and his sons, Hank and Tank, are super friendly and cook up some of the best barbecue you will ever have the pleasure of eating.

Open Seasonally
March–mid November
Thursday & Friday: 11:00 am to 8:00 pm
Saturday: 11:00 am to 8:00 pm (or until sold out)

Peanut Butter Bon Bons

1½ sticks butter, softened
1 cup peanut butter
1 (16-ounce) package powdered sugar
2 pounds chocolate, melted

Mix butter, peanut butter and powdered sugar together; shape into 1-inch balls. Dip in melted chocolate; place on wax paper until chocolate is set. Makes approximately 110 to 120 balls. Place in airtight container or zip-close bag. Can be frozen.

Family Favorite

Stuffed Mushrooms

2 cartons portobello mushrooms

1 cup Italian-style breadcrumbs

2 cups grated Parmesan cheese

½ pound imitation crab
sticks, finely cut

⅛ teaspoon pepper

¼ to ½ cup garlic wine vinegar

5 cloves garlic, minced

Olive oil

Monterey cheese, thin slices

1 stick butter, melted

Clean mushrooms and remove stems; drain. Chop up stems very fine. Mix stems, breadcrumbs, Parmesan, crabmeat, pepper and vinegar. Sauté garlic for 2 minutes in just enough olive oil to cover bottom of large skillet. Add crab mixture; stir over low heat for 15 minutes. Stuff mushroom caps with crab mixture. Place in a 9x13-inch baking dish; cover each mushroom with a slice of cheese. Pour butter over mushrooms. Bake at 350° for 25 to 30 minutes, making sure cheese is melted.

Family Favorite

Potato Bake

1 (16-ounce) carton sour cream

1 (8-ounce) package shredded
Cheddar cheese

1 (10.75-ounce) can cream
of chicken soup

1 cup chopped onions

1 (32-ounce) package frozen
southern-style hash browns, thawed

1 cup crushed cornflakes

2 tablespoons butter or
margarine, melted

Preheat oven to 375°. In a large bowl, combine sour cream, cheese, soup and onions. Add potatoes; mix well. Spoon into a greased 9x13-inch baking dish. Top with cornflakes and butter. Cover with foil. Bake for 35 minutes.

Family Favorite

Café Verona

206 West Lexington Avenue
Independence, MO 64050
816-833-0044
www.caféveronarestaurant.com

Whether meeting for a business lunch, gathering with friends, or dining for a special night out, Café Verona's menu includes dishes full of bold flavor and fresh ingredients. Try the salad bistecca, pistachio salmon, filet with mac-and-cheese, steak Florentine, or one of the many other tempting dishes on your next visit.

Monday–Thursday: 11:00 am to 9:00 pm
Friday & Saturday: 11:00 am to 10:00 pm

Meatballs

¼ cup extra virgin olive oil

2 medium yellow onions, chopped

¼ cup minced garlic

2 cups red wine

6 pounds ground beef

4 pounds medium Italian sausage

12 eggs, beaten

4 cups Italian breadcrumbs

3 tablespoons sugar

¼ cup kosher salt

4 tablespoons black pepper

2 tablespoons crushed
red pepper flakes

¼ cup Italian seasonings

3 tablespoons dried oregano leaves

2 cups grated Parmesan cheese

Heat large skillet with olive oil over medium heat; add onions and garlic, cooking until translucent. Add red wine; cook for 3 to 5 minutes. Once wine is reduced by half, remove from heat; cool. In a bowl, add ground beef, sausage, eggs, breadcrumbs, sugar, spices and cheese. Once onion garlic mix is cool, add to meat mixture. Using clean hands, work mixture to combine. Refrigerate mix overnight. Scoop mixture into 2-ounce balls onto clean sheet tray. Bake at 375° for 35 minutes. Once fully cooked, add to your favorite pasta; top with sauce and cheese.

Restaurant Recipe

FIRST PRESIDENTIAL LIBRARY

Harry S. Truman Presidential Library and Museum, Independence

One of only thirteen U.S. Presidential Libraries, and the first built under the provisions of the 1955 Presidential Libraries Act, the Harry S. Truman Library and Museum is the presidential library for Harry S. Truman, the 33rd president of the United States (1945–1953).

Built on a hill overlooking the Kansas City skyline, on land donated by the City of Independence, the Truman Library was dedicated July 6, 1957, in a ceremony which included the Masonic Rites of Dedication and attendance by former President Herbert Hoover (then the only living former president other than President Truman) and former First Lady Eleanor Roosevelt.

Two permanent exhibits chronicle the Missourian's private life and political career—with exhibits depicting his most difficult decisions, like using the atomic bomb, the Cold War and recognizing Israel. In an educational program called The White House Decision Center, school students take on the roles of President Truman and his advisors facing real-life historical decisions in a re-creation of the West Wing of the White House. The museum's historical collection consists of approximately 30,000 objects, including hundreds of Truman family possessions, political memorabilia, diplomatic gifts, and 1,300 letters from the Truman courtship and marriage.

President Truman and his wife, Bess, their daughter Margaret Truman Daniel, and her husband E. Clifton Daniel, are buried in the museum's courtyard. Museum visitors can also see two of Truman's offices—the actual office he used at the Library from 1957–1966 and a replica of his Oval Office with a recorded message from him about the contents. There are also exhibits featuring the guns used by the two Puerto Rican nationalists who almost killed Truman in 1950 and a copy of the 1948 "Dewey Defeats Truman" newspaper.

Dedicated in July 1957, the Harry S. Truman Library and Museum was the second Presidential Library to receive national designation but the first to be created under the 1955 Presidential Libraries Act. The Truman Library is administered by the National Archives and Records Administration and supported in part by its nonprofit partner, the Truman Library Institute.

Harry S. Truman Presidential Library and Museum
500 West US Highway 24
Independence, MO 64050
816-268-8200
www.trumanlibrary.org

FUN FACTS:

- On May 8, 1884, Harry S. Truman was born in Lamar, Missouri.

- On July 26, 1948, President Truman issued Executive Order 9981, establishing equality of treatment and opportunity in the Armed Services.

- Truman flew to Washington (state) on June 19, 1945, becoming the first president in office to use air travel within the country.

Truman Presidential
Museum & Library

The Courthouse Exchange

113 West Lexington Avenue
Independence, MO 64050
816-252-0344
www.courthouseexchange.com

The Court House Exchange, a casual pub where locals hang out and discuss news of the day, sports, politics, and civic matters, is located below street level with rock walls, wooden bar, and fixtures lending the bar a cozy feel. Try the burgers and fries, the fried chicken platter, or a hefty pork tenderloin. They keeps customers happy with down-home food with a friendly atmosphere. The menu includes daily specials such as meatloaf and fried liver dinners. The bar serves a selection of domestic, import, and microbrew beers, including hometown favorite, Boulevard. The Court House Exchange has been serving fine burgers since 1899.

Monday–Thursday: 11:00 am to 9:00 pm
Friday & Saturday: 11:00 am to 10:00 pm

Pork Tenderloin Sandwich

½ cup flour

Garlic powder, salt and pepper to taste

¼ cup 2% milk

½ cup buttermilk

1 (6-ounce) pork cutlet, flattened

Oil for frying

1 Kaiser bun, toasted

Mayonnaise

Horseradish

1 lettuce leaf

4 pickle chips

2 red onion rings

2 tomato slices

Season flour with garlic, salt and pepper; set aside. Mix together milk and buttermilk; set aside. Dip cutlet in seasoned flour, then in buttermilk mixture, and back in seasoned flour. Heat oil for frying to 350°; fry 4 minutes on each side or until golden brown. Place on bun bottom; top with mayonnaise, horseradish, lettuce, pickle chips, onion rings, tomato slices and bun top.

Restaurant Recipe

Ophelia's Restaurant and Inn

201 North Main Street
Independence, MO 64050
816-836-4004
www.opheliasind.com

Opening Ophelia's didn't happen because Ken and Cindy McClain wanted to own a restaurant, but instead because of a desire to revive the Independence Square. The Square is rich with Truman history and seemed a shame to waste. A restaurant seemed like a logical place to start because it can become a destination situation unlike other types of businesses. The desire to revive the Square has grown since they began this adventure. Above the upscale restaurant is a modern bed and breakfast in the center of Independence, President Harry Truman's hometown.

Monday–Thursday: 11:00 am to 9:00 pm
Friday & Saturday: 11:00 am to 10:00 pm
Sunday: 10:30 am to 2:30 pm

Crab Cakes

1 medium red onion, diced

1 red bell pepper, diced

1 yellow bell pepper, diced

½ cup breadcrumbs

2 eggs, beaten

¼ cup chopped cilantro,
plus more for garnish

2 teaspoons salt

2 teaspoons black pepper

3 tablespoons Old Bay Seasoning

1 tablespoon Sambal spice
(crushed red pepper paste)

1 (16-ounce) can lump crabmeat

Olive oil for sautéing

Sauté onion and pepper in a small sauté pan for 5 minutes or until translucent and golden brown. Combine pepper mix, breadcrumbs, eggs, cilantro and spices until well blended; add crab. Form cakes to your desired size. In a sauté pan, add olive oil to coat bottom of pan. Heat pan; add cakes. Cook 3 to 4 minutes on each side or until golden brown. Garnish with fresh cilantro.

Restaurant Recipe

BB's Lawnside BBQ

1205 East 85th Street
Kansas City, MO 64131
816-822-7427
www.bbslawnsidebbq.com

BB's Lawnside BBQ combines two great Kansas City traditions: blues and barbecue. For 25 years, BB's has served slow-smoked meats (burnt ends, ribs, pulled pork, beef brisket, chicken, and Italian sausage) from its more than 60-year-old pit. Plus, BB's menu includes signature Louisiana dishes such as gumbo, jambalaya, red beans and rice, and goulash. Popular BB's menu items such as the burnt ends, BBQ sundae, and Memphis Minnie's Smoked Catfish have been featured on Guy Fieri's *Diners, Drive-Ins and Dives* and Anthony Bourdain's *No Reservations*. Combine that with world-class blues music six nights a week, and you get a unique Kansas City experience only found at BB's Lawnside BBQ.

Tuesday: Kitchen 11:00 am to 10:00 pm
Wednesday: Kitchen 11:00 am to 9:00 pm
Thursday: Kitchen 11:00 am to 10:30 pm
Friday & Saturday: Kitchen 11:00 am to 11:00 pm
Sunday: Kitchen 11:00 am to 9:00 pm

BBQ Meatloaf

Unlike any other...ours is a blend of hickory smoked beef brisket and ground beef with a hint of sweet barbecue sauce. This is not your mom's meatloaf. The smoked brisket gives it a unique texture, and it tastes delicious with our homemade green beans and skillet fries.

1 pound smoked brisket, minced

1 pound ground chuck (80/20)

½ cup breadcrumbs

2 large eggs, beaten

¼ cup ketchup

¼ cup BB's Sweet Mild BBQ Sauce, plus more for glazing

1 medium onion, diced

1 medium green bell pepper, diced

½ teaspoon salt

½ teaspoon pepper

½ teaspoon garlic powder

1 tablespoon Worcestershire sauce

Combine all ingredients until well incorporated. Bake in a greased 9x5-inch loaf pan at 350° for 45 minutes, or internal temperature of meatloaf is 165°. Glaze with additional barbeque sauce; cool 10 minutes.

Family Recipe

BC Bistro

7749 Northwest Prairie View Road
Kansas City, MO 64151
816-587-0899
www.bcbistrokc.com

BC Bistro offers creative, made-from-scratch meals alongside crafty cocktails and great wines. Chef owner Brent Mattison and his wife Coley focused on a bistro-theme for their restaurant so they could combine a variety of cuisines into one outstanding menu. You will love appetizers like shrimp and crab dip made with smoked gouda and the BC Salad with honey citrus marinated chicken with sunflower seeds, dried cranberries and goat cheese. There are many sandwich options including the salmon avocado club served on fresh berry wheat bread and pasta dishes like Cajun tortellini-chicken and shrimp sauteed with peppers and onions, cheese-filled tortellini and a Cajun cream sauce. That Mattison's ultimate goal is to be known for offering great food and drinks that keep everyone craving more.

Tuesday–Thursday: 11:00 am to 9:00 pm
Friday & Saturday: 11:00 am to 10:00 pm
Sunday; Brunch only 10:00 am to 2:00 pm

Missouri Peach Streusel Cheesecake

Crust:

25 graham crackers, crushed

½ cup sugar

3 tablespoons butter, melted

Preheat oven to 350° with a water bath (pan with water under baking surface). Line a 10-inch spring form pan with liner. In a medium bowl, mix graham cracker crumbs, sugar and butter; press onto bottom of pan. Bake 10 minutes; cool.

Peach Mix:

10 peaches

½ pound butter

¼ cup brown sugar

½ cup honey

¼ teaspoon cinnamon

1 teaspoon vanilla

Pinch salt

Peel and slice peaches; set aside. In a saucepan over medium heat, melt butter; while continually stirring, add brown sugar, honey, cinnamon and vanilla, mixing well. Add peaches; simmer on low heat 10 minutes. Season with a pinch of salt. Allow Peach Mix to cool.

Cheesecake:

1 cup sugar

1 tablespoon vanilla

1 teaspoon salt

1 teaspoon cinnamon

3 (8-ounce) packages cream cheese, softened

3 eggs

In large bowl using an electric mixer, combine sugar, vanilla, salt and cinnamon; blend 1 minute. Slowly add cream cheese to mixture until blended well; add eggs, 1 at a time. Once smooth, add 1 cup Peach Mix, setting the rest aside for topping. Pour filling into prepared crust. Bake at 350° for 5 minutes. Reduce heat to 225°; bake 2 hours. Cheesecake should be slightly jiggly but firm. Cool completely before topping.

Streusel Topping:

½ cup flour

½ cup brown sugar

½ cup oats

2 tablespoons butter, softened

Pinch cinnamon

Pinch salt

In medium bowl, mix flour, brown sugar, and oats. Using your hands, work in butter gently, leaving clumps. Spread out on a sheet pan; bake 350° for 10 minutes. Stir mixture; bake an additional 10 minutes. Top with warm peach mix and streusel topping. Serve with vanilla ice cream.

Restaurant Recipe

District.Pour House + Kitchen

7122 Wornall Road
Kansas City, MO 64114
816-333-0799
www.districtpourhousekc.com

District. Pour House + Kitchen in Historic Waldo offers unique craft brews and libations, original American food, and local flair. They feature 34 infused spirits, including 3 rotating, seasonal selections, 100 bottled beers, and 13 on draught. The Libations menu is crafted around the infusions, using only the finest and freshest ingredients. The food menu is New, Progressive American cuisine by Chef John Magno, highlighting flavors from multiple regions to satisfy everyone's cravings. This place is upscale, yet casual, romantic, but edgy—a place you can visit for your first date or to watch the big game with all your buddies. Both owners, Jason Rourke and Dan McCall, are local with a love and inspiration of their neighborhood.

Monday–Friday: 11:00 am to 1:30 am
Saturday: 10:00 am to 1:30 am
Sunday: 10:00 am to 12:00 am

District Mussels

1 pound mussels, live or frozen

¼ cup olive oil

1 ounce diced prosciutto or bacon

1 medium shallot, minced

1 garlic clove, minced

1 small pear, thinly sliced

1 sprig rosemary

½ teaspoon kosher salt

¼ teaspoon fresh-cracked black pepper

¼ cup white wine

½ cup heavy cream

1 tablespoon butter

1 teaspoon stone ground mustard

Rinse the mussels in cold water to remove grit; strain. Discard opened mussels. In a medium sauté pan, heat olive oil on medium-high heat; cook bacon or prosciutto until slightly crisp. Add the shallot, garlic, pear, rosemary, salt and pepper; cook 2 minutes. Add white wine, heavy cream, butter, mustard and mussels. Cover pan; cook on medium-high heat for 6 minutes or until all the mussels are open. (Optional: for a creamier sauce, remove mussels from the pan and reduce the liquid until desired consistency is reached.)

Restaurant Recipe

District Chimichurri

This sauce is very simple to make and goes well on everything—fried goat cheese, grilled steak, pork tenderloin and seafood.

1 cup parsley

⅓ cup red wine vinegar

1 cup cilantro leaves

2 garlic cloves

1 pinch crushed red pepper

1 pinch cumin

1 teaspoon salt

1 jalapeño, seeded

1 shallot

½ cup olive oil

In a food processor or blender, purée parsley, red wine vinegar, cilantro, garlic, red pepper, cumin, salt, jalapeño and shallot; slowly add olive oil while blender is running. Season to taste. For a rustic style chimichurri, hand-cut ingredients. Put everything in an airtight container; shake vigorously for a couple minutes.

Restaurant Recipe

FROM RIVER DISASTER TO BURIED TREASURE TO WORLD-RENOWNED MUSEUM

Arabia Steamboat Museum, Kansas City

It's a fascinating series of events. A steamboat sinks on the Missouri River in 1856. Over time, the river changes course and the location of the sunken ship becomes a cornfield. Then, in 1987, three men set out to find the lost ship. It is a modern-day treasure-hunt culminating in the creation of the Arabia Steamboat Museum and a story for the ages.

In September 1856, the *Arabia* was carrying over 200 tons of cargo intended for general stores and homes in 16 midwestern frontier towns. The steamer was still fully loaded when it hit a tree snag and sank just 6 miles west of Kansas City. Due to erosion, the Missouri River changed course over time, and the *Arabia* was buried underground for over a century—along with its precious cargo.

In 1987, using a metal detector and old maps to guide the search, an amateur archaeologist, Bob Hawley and his two sons, began the adventure of a lifetime. They discovered the lost steamer a half-mile from the present river's course, lying 45-feet deep beneath a Kansas cornfield.

The owners of the farm gave permission for excavation, so the Hawleys, along with family friends Jerry Mackey and David Luttrell, set out to excavate the *Arabia*. Heavy equipment, including a 100-ton crane, was brought in along with 20 irrigation pumps that were installed around the site to lower the water level and to keep the site from flooding. The 65-foot deep wells removed 20,000 gallons of water per minute from the ground.

On November 26, 1988, the *Arabia* was exposed. Four days later, artifacts from it began to appear, beginning with a Goodyear rubber overshoe. On December 5, a wooden crate filled with elegant china was unearthed. The mud was such an effective preserver that the yellow packing straw was still visible. Thousands of artifacts were recovered intact, including jars of preserved food that are still edible.

The artifacts were lovingly and carefully recovered and are housed in the Arabia Steamboat Museum, providing visitors a one-of-a-kind opportunity to experience the everyday objects that made life possible for pioneers in the 1800's. Still run by the Hawley family, it is the largest single collection of pre-Civil War artifacts in the world.

Arabia Steamboat Museum
400 Grand Blvd
Kansas City, MO 64106
816-471-4030
www.1856.com

FUN FACTS:

- The Mighty Missouri, as it was often called, is the longest river in the United States and has claimed nearly 400 other steamboats over its 2,500-mile course.

- The *Arabia's* paddle wheels were 28 feet across, and its steam boilers consumed approximately 30 cords of wood per day.

- Built in the boatyard of John S. Pringle in 1853, she would survive only three years of service on the shallow and unpredictable western-river system.

- In addition to its 200-ton cargo, there were about 130 passengers aboard bound for a new life on the frontier.

- When work ceased at the excavation site, and the pumps were turned off, the hole filled with water overnight.

- In November, 1991, the Arabia Steamboat Museum opened its doors to the public.

il Lazzarone

412 Delaware Street
Kansas City, MO 64105
816-541-3695
www.illazzarone.org

il Lazzarone (pronounced "lazza'roni") is a family-owned pizzeria. The lazzaroni were the street folk of Naples, who in essence invented pizza. It is said that when a lazzaroni had worked long enough to afford a Neapolitan pizza and a bottle of wine, he was done working for the day. il lazzarone embodies the true Italian spirit of relaxation and community. Using only the highest quality ingredients and following the law of traditional Neapolitan wood-fired pizza by using only four simple ingredients in the dough and cooking the pizza in under 90 seconds, il Lazzarone is one of 77 locations in the entire United States with official certification.

Monday–Saturday: 11:00 am to 1:30 am
Sunday: 11:00 am to 12:00 am

Bruschetta

2 tomatoes, medium diced

¼ cup finely chopped garlic

½ cup rough-chopped basil

¼ cup extra virgin olive oil (evoo)

2 tablespoons fine sea salt

1 cup balsamic vinegar

2 cups sugar

1 dough ball

1 whole basil leaf

In a bowl, combine tomatoes with garlic, basil, evoo, and sea salt. Let marinate for 2 hours. On low heat, combine vinegar and sugar. Let sit on low for 2 hours or until it reaches your desired thickness. (It should reduce down to a glaze.) Stretch dough ball out to approximately 2x6 inches or the size of a loaf of bread. Thickness should be between ⅛ and ¼ inch thick. Bake bread in 500°-degree oven for approximately 8 minutes or until golden brown. Cut bread into ½-inch squares. Top with tomato mixture. Drizzle desired amount of balsamic glaze on top; garnish with basil leaf. Serves 4.

Restaurant Recipe

Frito Mascarpone

1 dough ball

1 cup mascarpone cheese (softened)

4 tablespoons honey (more or less)

Powdered sugar to taste

¼ cup whipped cream

Stretch dough ball into approximately 2x6-inch long oval cut into strips. In a sauté pan or tabletop fryer, fry dough to golden brown and cooked through. Put cheese into pastry bag and pipe onto fried dough. Top with desired amount of honey; dust with powdered sugar. Pipe with 2 dollops of whipped cream and serve. Serves 4.

Restaurant Recipe

Stroud's
Oak Ridge Manor

5410 Northeast Oak Ridge Drive
Kansas City, MO 64119
816-454-9600
www.stroudsnorth.com
Find us on Facebook

In 1983, Mike and Dennis Donegan, along with Jim Hogan, purchased Oak Ridge Manor, continuing the tradition that began in 1933—serving award-winning food and receiving the recognition they so justly earned. Stroud's has received many national awards, including the James Beard Award for Excellence and the Zagat Award for Best Restaurant, as well as being featured on many national television shows. Mike, the surviving owner, and the caring professional staff, operate Stroud's with the ultimate goal of serving home-cooked meals in a friendly atmosphere.

Monday–Thursday: 5:00 pm to 9:30 pm
Friday: 11:00 am to 10:00 pm
Saturday: 2:00 pm to 10:00 pm
Sunday: 11:00 am to 9:30 pm

Stroud's Brownies

6 cups all-purpose flour

6 cups sugar

1 tablespoon cinnamon

2 tablespoons baking soda

8 eggs

1½ cups buttermilk

3 tablespoons vanilla

1½ pounds butter

1½ cups water

1½ cups cocoa

In a large mixing bowl, combine flour, sugar, cinnamon, baking soda, eggs, buttermilk and vanilla; mix well. In a saucepan, melt butter; add water and cocoa. Pour cocoa mixture into flour mixture; blend well. Grease and flour 2 large foil pans; pour in mixture. Bake at 325° for 30 to 40 minutes. Ice brownies while still warm.

Icing:

¾ pound butter

1 cup milk

1½ cups cocoa

3 tablespoons vanilla

3½ pounds powdered sugar

Melt butter; add milk and cocoa. Stir in powdered sugar. Pour over finished brownies; cool.

Restaurant Recipe

Chicken-Noodle Soup

6 chicken thighs

3 carrots, diced

¼ cup fresh parsley

4 cups canned chicken stock

4 cups water

2 eggs

¼ teaspoon salt

1½ cups flour, divided

Salt and pepper to taste

Dash Worcestershire sauce

Simmer thighs, carrots and parsley in chicken stock and water 45 to 60 minutes, or until chicken meat is very tender. Remove chicken from stock, pull meat from bones and return meat to pot. Remove pot from heat. In a mixing bowl, beat eggs and salt until smooth. Beat in ⅔ cup flour, then continue adding flour, up to a total of 1½ cups, until a pliable dough is formed. Knead dough 5 minutes on a lightly floured board. Roll about ¹⁄₁₆-inch thick and use a sharp knife to cut into ½-inch wide noodles, 2 inches long. Roll and cut scraps. Return soup to stove; bring to a simmer. Add noodles, salt, pepper and Worcestershire sauce. Simmer 7 to 10 minutes or until noodles are cooked through and tender. Yields 4 servings.

Restaurant Recipe

Morning Day Café

6 East Franklin Street
Liberty, MO 64068
816-883-8258
www.morningdaycafé.com

Opened in July 2014, Morning Day Café is an artsy, quirky café, coffee shop, and breakfast pub that's focused on creating food that's natural, unprocessed, chemical-free, and locally sourced. They keep it fresh and offer options for most allergies. Come savor a bottomless cup of organic, locally-roasted coffee, or order your favorite espresso drink, smoothie, tea, or cocktail from the full bar. Open for breakfast and lunch, Morning Day serves unique entrées, sandwiches, and salads made with ingredients that are natural, chemical-free, unprocessed, and sourced locally. The menu offers items for their gluten-free, dairy-free, vegetarian, and vegan friends. So, come sit a spell.

7 days a week: 6:00 am to 4:00 pm
Nite Bites Friday & Saturday: 4:00 pm till late

Whole-Wheat Pancakes

1 cup organic whole-wheat flour

½ teaspoon baking soda

1 teaspoon baking powder

1 egg, beaten

1 cup milk

½ cup natural yogurt (any flavor)

1 teaspoon vanilla

Mix dry ingredients; add wet ingredients. Stir well; in a lightly greased skillet over medium heat until bubbles appear on top, then flip and cook until browned and set in the middle. Stuff with berries or chocolate chips for extra yum.

Restaurant Recipe

Organic Cinnamon Syrup

2 cups water

3 organic cinnamon sticks

2 cups raw organic sugar

1 vanilla bean, split, scraped

Add all ingredients to saucepan; bring to a boil. Simmer 5 minutes each day for 5 days. Allow mixture to rest in pan between heatings. Add to coffee, hot chocolate, ice cream and desserts.

Restaurant Recipe

WONDER DOG OR FORTUNE TELLER?
Jim The Wonder Dog Memorial Park, Marshall

By all accounts, Jim was a magical dog who could understand words and even predict the future. And, in case you have your doubts, it was all proven in a special session of the Missouri State Legislature.

Jim was the runt of a pureblood litter of LLewellyn Setters and was purchased—at half the price of his siblings—by Sam Van Arsdale who worked with a trainer to teach Jim to hunt. Jim spent most of his time laying in the shade showing very little promise as a hunting dog during his training. It seems that he was paying attention. Once tested in the field, Jim proved to be an outstanding hunting dog, finding quail, holding steady until it was shot, and acting on Van Arsdale's command of fetch immediately. He was so outstanding that he was called "The Hunting Dog of the Country" by Outdoor Life Magazine.

One day, the two were hunting when Sam said, "Let's sit in the shade of that hickory tree and rest." Jim trotted over to a hickory tree and sat down. Intrigued, Sam told him to find an oak tree. Jim did. Then he found a walnut tree, a cedar, an ordinary stump and even a hazel bush. Sam was becoming aware that Jim was more than an ordinary dog.

Jim's amazing abilities didn't stop there. It is said he could find a specific car with a specific license plate number, or a car by color or from another state. He could also pick out, from a crowd, specific people of the community, whether they knew Jim or not. And at the height of his talents, Jim the Wonder Dog could predict the future. He chose the winner of the Kentucky Derby seven years in a row, predicted the Yankee victory in the 1936 baseball World Series and correctly identified the sex of unborn infants.

After testing Jim, the director of the School of Veterinary Medicine, Dr. A. J. Durant, said Jim "possessed an occult power that might never come again to a dog in many generations."

Jim was invited to Jefferson City to demonstrate his powers before a joint session of the Missouri Legislature. He picked out various people from their complexions and from certain types and colors of dress. He obeyed an order given him in shorthand. In order to preclude any secret signaling, a Morse code message was tapped out (Sam didn't understand Morse code) instructing Jim to walk to a certain member. Jim did it.

In 1999, Jim the Wonder Dog Memorial Park was built in Marshall in Jim's honor. With manicured plantings and shrubs and surrounded by old brick buildings, it is a restful and beautiful place to stop. A brick walkway takes you past a gazebo and over a trickling brook past plaque stations that describe Jim's amazing life and achievements. At the center is a statue of Jim.

Jim the Wonder Dog Memorial Park
101 North Lafayette
Marshall, MO 65340
www.jimthewonderdog.org

FUN FACTS:

- Sam was constantly worried that gambling interests would steal his amazing dog. In order to keep Jim nearby, Sam turned down a $364,000 offer from Paramount and another lucrative offer from a dog food company.

- Jim's favorite food was cornbread.

- A request from the University of Missouri for Jim's brains was denied.

- Jim the Wonder Dog was featured in Ripley's Believe it or Not.

- It seemed that Jim could do everything well. For this reason, he was insured for $100,000 against accident.

- He was the most famous hunting dog of the 20th century — during his career more than 5,000 birds were shot over him.

- Jim passed away at the age of 12 on March 18, 1937 and was buried just outside of Ridge Park Cemetery in Marshall.

- Sam wanted Jim buried in the family plot in the cemetery, but authorities would not permit this, so he was buried just outside the cemetery gate. Ironically, the cemetery has since been enlarged and Jim's grave is now within its boundaries.

- Officials report that more people visit Jim's grave more than any other in the cemetery.

JIM THE WONDER DOG
1925 — 1937

Down Home Café

119 South 2nd Street
Odessa, MO 64076
816-633-7227

Ever hear people talk about a place where the cooks know what they are doing? They are probably talking about Down Home Café in Odessa. Come join owner, Jennifer and the gang. They are there to make your tummy happy, not to mention full as a tick with the huge portions they dish out. You'll enjoy down-home recipes like your mother and grandma cooked—eggs; just the way you like them, bacon crispy, and mouth-watering tender breakfast steak. Don't forget the plate-sized pancakes, so light and fluffy they almost float off the plate. This is just breakfast. Can you imagine what lunch is like?

7 days a week 6:00 am to 2:00 pm

Cheesy Corn

1 (16-ounce) package frozen
whole-kernel corn

1 tablespoon chopped fresh parsley

1 teaspoon chopped garlic

½ teaspoon Creole seasoning

4 tablespoons butter

⅓ cup diced onion

1 (8-ounce) package cream cheese

In a saucepan over medium heat, combine corn, parsley, garlic and Creole seasoning. Add water to cover; bring to a boil. Reduce heat to medium and cook until corn is tender, about 20 minutes. Drain and set aside. Melt butter in a large skillet over medium heat; sauté onions just until tender (do not brown). Add corn and cream cheese. Reduce heat to low and cook about 10 minutes. Serve hot, or this recipe is also delicious chilled and served cold.

Local Favorite

Peach Turnovers

3 large peaches, peeled and pitted

2 (8-ounce) cans crescent rolls

2 sticks butter

1½ cups sugar

1 teaspoon vanilla extract

½ teaspoon salt

½ (12-ounce) bottle Mountain Dew

1 pinch ground cinnamon

Preheat oven to 350°. Slice peaches and set aside. Working on a flat surface, unroll crescent dough and separate into 16 triangles. Place a peach slice at the base of each triangle and roll up. Arrange in a 9x13-inch pan as you work. Melt butter in a small saucepan over medium-low heat. Whisk in sugar, vanilla and salt. Pour around turnovers in baking pan. Pour Mountain Dew over turnovers. Sprinkle cinnamon on top. Bake 30 to 40 minutes, or until turnovers are golden brown and liquid is bubbling.

Local Favorite

Cook's Corner Café

203 US Highway 169
Smithville, MO 64089
816-343-2118
Find us on Facebook

With a love of cooking in her blood, Cami Wagers bought Cook's Corner Café from her mother and aunt to make her dream of owning her own restaurant come true. Cami wanted to bring new items into the café, but soon learned that her customers still wanted their cheeseburgers and tenderloins, which are among the top sellers. Cami still looks after all her customers by offering healthier options like lemon pepper grilled fish, buffalo chicken wraps, soup-of-the-day, and entrée salads.

Sunday–Tuesday: 7:00 am to 3:00 pm
Wednesday–Saturday: 7:00 am to 8:00 pm

Coconut Pie

Makes its own crust.

½ cup self-rising flour
1¾ cups sugar
2 cups milk
4 eggs, beaten
1½ cups flaked coconut
1 teaspoon vanilla

In a bowl, combine all ingredients; mix well. Pour in well-greased glass pie plate; bake at 300° for 45 to 60 minutes until golden brown.

Local Favorite

Toasted Ravioli

Cooking oil as needed
50 uncooked ravioli
1½ cups breadcrumbs
½ cup grated Parmesan cheese

In a skillet, heat oil to 375°. Coat ravioli with breadcrumbs; deep-fry in small batches 2 to 3 minutes until golden brown. Remove ravioli to drain. While still warm, sprinkle with Parmesan cheese. Serve with tomato and mushroom sauce for dipping.

Local Favorite

Bunk House Bar & Grill

17965 Highway 45
Weston, MO 64098
816-640-0000
Find us on Facebook

The building that is now known as the Bunk House Bar & Grill was originally built in the 1950's as a bunkhouse for the migrant workers at Hall's Orchard. The bunkhouse was first opened as a bar in the early 1990's and although it has changed ownership over the years, the Bunk House continues as a bar and grill today. Owner and local Weston resident, Rachel Jackson, invites you to come enjoy the casual atmosphere, friendly service, and great food prepared fresh for your dine-in or carry-out order. Other amenities include a full-service bar, jukebox, pool table, darts, outdoor patio, WiFi, and multiple TV's to watch your favorite sporting event.

Bar Hours
Monday–Saturday: 11:00 am to 1:30 am
Grill Hours
Monday–Thursday: 11:00 am to 8:00 pm
Friday & Saturday: 11:00 am to 9:00 pm

The Blue Jay Burger

1¼ tablespoons minced, sautéed garlic

½ cup blue cheese crumbles

1 (8-ounce) package cream
cheese, softened

8 beef patties, uncooked

4 large sourdough buns, toasted

Cream together garlic, blue cheese and cream cheese. Starting with 1 patty, top it with 1½ tablespoons cream cheese mixture; pinch seams together to seal. Repeat with remaining patties. Grill until cooked thoroughly. Serve on toasted buns with your favorite toppings.

Restaurant Recipe

The Mother Clucker

5 (12-inch) flour tortillas

Ranch dressing

1 cup shredded lettuce

½ cup diced tomatoes

8 to 12 slices bacon, cooked

8 breaded or grilled chicken strips

1 cup shredded Cheddar cheese

Lightly grill 4 tortillas. Cut 1 tortilla in strips; deep-fry. Spread ranch dressing over 4 tortillas. Top with lettuce, tomatoes, bacon, chicken, tortilla strips and cheese. Roll filled tortilla, tucking in sides. Serve.

Restaurant Recipe

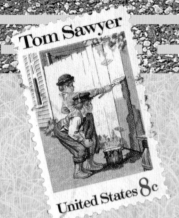

63

Bishop's Post

16125 Chesterfield Parkway West
Chesterfield, MO 63017
636-536-9404
www.bishopspost.com

Our seasonal menu includes fresh seafood, hand-cut steaks, homemade pasta, house-smoked shrimp and trout, artisan cheeses, and charcuterie. We also offer exquisite comfort food options that include our macaroni and cheese with beef tenderloin and St. Louis-style ribs. Our salads use the farm-to-table philosophy, including sourcing herbs and vegetables from our on-site garden. Our wine list includes more than 200 old and new world wines.

Monday–Thursday: 11:00 am to 9:00 pm
Friday & Saturday: 11:00 am to 10:00 pm
Bar remains open an hour later every day.

Apple and Golden Raisin Chutney

Best served with roasted poultry or pork. Goes great with cheese dishes as well.

5 apples, peeled and diced

½ cup dried golden raisins

1 red onion, diced

1 teaspoon minced fresh ginger

1 orange, zested

1 lemon, zested

½ teaspoon minced garlic

1 tablespoon balsamic vinegar

5 ounces brown sugar

Combine all ingredients in a thick-bottomed saucepan. Simmer over low heat, stirring occasionally, until a syrup-like texture forms. Chill.

Restaurant Recipe

Seafood Campechana

½ quart Clamato juice

¼ cup fresh lime juice

1 tablespoon chopped fresh oregano

1 jalapeño, grilled or roasted,
cooled, seeded and diced

1 tablespoon chopped fresh parsley

½ cup ketchup

¼ cup chopped green olives

1 cup diced tomatoes

½ cup diced yellow onion

¼ cup chopped cilantro

½ cup diced avocado

½ tablespoon chopped garlic

½ cup orange juice

6 (21- to 25-count) cocktail
shrimp, chopped large

4 ounces super or jumbo
lump crabmeat

Combine all ingredients. Serve with corn tortilla chips or crackers.

Restaurant Recipe

Bishop's Post Chicken Salad

This has been a staple at the restaurant for years. It is our own take on a classic dish and goes great on a croissant to make a sandwich.

2 (6-ounce) roasted chicken
breasts, cooled and hand pulled

1 cup mayonnaise

4 stalks celery, diced

¼ cup chopped parsley

¼ cup honey

1 teaspoon fresh lime juice

½ teaspoon Tabasco sauce

½ cup sour cream

½ cup dried cranberries

½ cup chopped pecans or walnuts

1 teaspoon salt

1 teaspoon black pepper

1 teaspoon granulated garlic

1 teaspoon Worcestershire sauce

Mix all ingredients.

Restaurant Recipe

A GIANT AWAKENING

The Awakening Sculpture, Chesterfield

Behind a mall, outside a park, in a pretty green grassy area, you will find…a 70-foot-tall giant clawing his way out of the ground? Yes.

The *Awakening* was installed on October 19, 2009, and is owned by Sachs Properties. This monumental sculpture, measuring 70 feet in length and 17 feet at its tallest point was first cast by sculptor Seward Johnson in 1980 for a sculpture exhibition in Washington, DC. This second casting is a permanent addition to the Chesterfield landscape adjacent to Central Park to the west of Chesterfield Mall.

Undeniably eye-catching, the 4,100-pound struggling sculpture is part of Chesterfield Arts' public art collection. The five-piece aluminum sculpture is buried in the ground, giving the impression of a distressed giant attempting to free himself from the ground. The left hand and right foot barely protrude, while the bent left leg and knee jut into the air. The bearded face, with the mouth in mid-scream, struggles to emerge from the earth.

Central Park
16365 Lydia Hill Drive
Chesterfield, MO 63017
www.chesterfield.mo.us/the-awakening.html

MORE INTERESTING SCULPTURES IN THE CHESTERFIELD AREA:

- Missouri Botanical Gardens Butterfly House is home to a super-large butterfly and monstrously oversized caterpillar. www.missouribotanicalgarden.org

- *Maura*—a beautiful bronze sculpture created by Don Wiegand—depicts a young girl running with her shadow behind her. Every year on June 26 at 10:00 am, her actual shadow meets her sculpted shadow in an amazing demonstration of nature and art. *Maura* is located at Chesterfield's Central Park near the entrance of the Family Aquatic Center.

- Also in Chesterfield's Central Park is *The Fox*, a life-size bronze sculpture depicting the life of a young fox leaping through the tall grass and running next to the trees.

FUN FACT:

The original version of *the Awakening* made its home in Washington DC for 27 years before being sold to developer Milton Peterson for $750,000 in 2007. The body parts were dug up and driven on three flatbed trucks to a man-made beach at National Harbor in Maryland.

The Awakening is the second casting of a 1980 sculpture by J. Seward Johnson of a 70-foot tall giant clawing his way out of the ground.

PM BBQ

161 Long Road
Chesterfield, MO 63005
636-536-1966
www.pmbbq.com

PM BBQ serves authentic, hickory-smoked barbecue, made-from-scratch side dishes, and fresh-baked desserts, all from treasured family recipes. With roots in Tennessee and Kentucky, owners Paul and Mark (PM), have perfected spice rubs for each of the meats that are smoked fresh at their restaurant every day. The side dishes are a nod to their wives, mothers, and grandmothers' ability to feed their families simple and tasty food. Made-from-scratch pies, cakes, and cookies are baked and served every day in their warm, inviting dining room. PM BBQ brings a touch of home to every meal.

Monday–Saturday: 11:00 am to 9:00 pm

Blue Ribbon Chicken Rub

4 cups sugar
½ cup paprika
1 tablespoon chili powder
1 teaspoon cayenne pepper
1 cup table salt
1 tablespoon coarse-ground black pepper
2 teaspoons granulated garlic

Combine all ingredients in a medium bowl. Stir until thoroughly mixed; store in an airtight container.

To use, sprinkle liberally on all sides of chicken. Refrigerate 1 hour or up to overnight before grilling.

Restaurant Recipe

Georgia Lee's Tart and Tangy Slaw

3 cups shredded cabbage

1 small yellow onion, chopped

1 medium green bell pepper, chopped

¾ cup sugar, divided

¾ cup white vinegar

1 teaspoon salt

1 teaspoon yellow mustard

1 teaspoon celery seed

⅛ teaspoon coarse-ground black pepper

½ cup salad oil

In a large bowl, combine cabbage, onions, green pepper and ½ cup sugar. Let stand for 10 to 15 minutes. In a medium saucepan, add vinegar, ¼ cup sugar, salt, mustard, celery seed, black pepper and oil; bring to a boil. Reduce heat slightly and continue to boil, uncovered, for 3 minutes. Pour over slaw mix; toss thoroughly. Refrigerate at least 1 hour before serving.

Restaurant Recipe

Aunt Candy's Smoked Chicken Salad

1 pound Blue Ribbon Smoked Chicken, deboned and coarsely shredded

1 medium Granny Smith Apple, peeled and diced

2 stalks celery, diced

½ cup mayonnaise

¼ cup sour cream

2 ounces cream cheese, softened

½ teaspoon salt

½ teaspoon coarse-ground black pepper

1 teaspoon Blue Ribbon Chicken Rub

½ teaspoon dill weed

1 tablespoon fresh lemon juice

½ cup chopped pecans

Chill smoked chicken. In a large bowl, combine all ingredients, except chicken. Mix thoroughly. Fold in the chilled, shredded chicken. Refrigerate at least 1 hour. Serve on toasted country white bread or on a bed of lettuce.

Restaurant Recipe

Becky Thatcher's Diner

213 North Third Street
Hannibal, MO 63401
573-719-3602
Becky Thatcher's Diner on Facebook

Becky Thatcher's Diner has been a Hannibal landmark for more than 50 years. Under new ownership, "The Diner" has undergone a complete renovation that will take you back to the '50s. Retro setting and tables, complete with original countertop and stools, are surrounded with checkerboard flooring. The menu features traditional diner fare, prepared from scratch with fresh ingredients. Breakfast all day includes specialty omelets and the best sausage gravy and sausage sandwich in the Midwest, if not the country. Burgers, tenderloins, sandwiches, and a signature Reuben all start with in-house roasted and hand-cut meats.

Monday–Saturday: 6:00 am to 2:00 pm
Sunday: 8:00 am to 2:00 pm

Chicken Cordon Blue Quiche

2 boneless chicken breasts
1 cup milk
2 cups all-purpose flour
½ cup Cavender's Greek Seasoning
12 eggs, beaten
1 teaspoon salt
1 teaspoon pepper
1 cup cream
½ cup shredded smoked Gouda cheese
½ cup shredded Swiss cheese
½ pound ham, finely chopped
1 unbaked pie crust

Soak chicken in milk 1 minute. Mix together flour and Cavender's; dredge chicken in flour mixture. Fry in hot oil in skillet until browned on both sides; chop into bite-size pieces. In a large bowl, mix eggs, salt, pepper, cream, cheese, ham and chicken together. Pour into pie crust. Bake at 375° for 45 minutes or until done.

Restaurant Recipe

Cuban Omelet

3 eggs
1 tablespoon water
Pinch salt and pepper
Roasted pork loin, shredded
Smoked Gouda
Ham, thin-sliced and chopped
1 pickle, chopped

Whisk together eggs, water, salt and pepper. In an omelet pan, add egg mixture; cook both sides. In another pan, heat meats with cheese layered between, until cheese melts. Add to egg mixture; fold. Top with Hollandaise Sauce and pickles.

Hollandaise Sauce:

6 egg yolks
2 tablespoons lemon juice
½ teaspoon salt
Pinch cayenne pepper
1 cup unsalted butter, melted and warm

In a blender, on high speed, blend yolks, lemon juice, salt and cayenne until well blended. Turn blender to medium speed; drizzle in butter. Blend just until incorporated.

Restaurant Recipe

A HAUNTED TOWN FOR YOUR HAUNTING PLEASURE

Haunted Ghost Tours, Hannibal

Whether you are a professional or amateur ghost hunter or a total skeptic, you are still sure to enjoy the Haunted Ghost Tours by Ken and Lisa Marks as you experience one of the most haunted towns in America.

You will enjoy a spine-tingling, guided driving tour to learn the secrets of many of Hannibal's most notoriously haunted sites, learn about Hannibal's rich history, and experience legends and ghost stories told and retold for more than 150 years. Hear stories of murder and mischief that took place during Mark Twain's boyhood days in Hannibal; meet the present-day ghosts of the mansions on Millionaire's Row; and visit other ghostly sites, including a visit to the Old Baptist Cemetery.

The highlight of the tour, you are given dousing rods to help you search for signs of paranormal activity among the graves—as old as the early 1800s—of slaves and Civil War soldiers. People have found stones with their name on them, graves of people who died the same day of the tour, or the death date of a beloved family member.

There are many stories from people who report seeing ghosts in the cemetery. Lisa, who never sees ghosts herself, says it is amazing how she hears the same "ghost story" over and over again from guests. Some of those include a five-year-old-girl playing peek-a-boo in the northwest corner of the cemetery; a man near the west fence line, very tall, dark, wearing a long overcoat; a Civil War soldier who is wearing his hat; and a man named Edward in the northeast part of the cemetery who isn't hostile, but not particularly friendly.

Haunted Ghost Tours depart from:

Hannibal History Museum
200 North Main Street
Hannibal, MO 63401
573-248-1819
www.HannibalHistoryMuseum.com

JUST A FEW HAUNTED SITES IN HANNIBAL:

Lula Belle's—A one-time bordello opened in 1917 that is now a bed and breakfast and restaurant. The haunts here are known to move or throw things in the kitchen, or twist utensils into pretzels.

Garth Woodside Mansion—This inn, built originally in 1871, is known for its connection with renowned author Mark Twain. Folks believe his ghost still visits the place.

Rockcliffe Mansion—A historic house museum and bed and breakfast where caretakers have reported seeing the indention of a man's body rumpling the bed linens in the bedroom of the house's original owner.

Built in 1875, it was originally the home of the First Congregational Church before being consecrated in 1880 for use by the Catholics. Numerous people have reported hearing organ music, choral singing, and the voices of priests.

Swiss Meat & Sausage Co.

2056 South Highway 19
Hermann, MO 65041
573-486-2086
www.swissmeats.com
Find us on Facebook

In the quaint village of Swiss, the heart of wine country, visit Swiss Meat & Sausage Company, founded in 1969 by Bill and the late Margie Sloan. Swiss has grown from a small family owned and operated butcher shop to a "Sausage Showroom," featuring more than 80 varieties of brats, some of which you'll find on the daily menu. Enjoy infamous pit-smoked beef brisket and pulled pork, along with Margie's famed German potato salad. They offer daily plate specials, as well as other entrées, sides, homemade soups, and desserts. After lunch, shop to your heart's content. Bring your cooler along. You don't want to pass up purchasing some of the best bratwurst and smoked meats in the state.

Monday–Saturday: 8:00 am to 5:00 pm
Sunday: 11:00 am to 4:00 pm Easter till Christmas

Margie's German Potato Salad

5 pounds potatoes, peeled and cubed

1 pound Swiss Meats
hickory-smoked bacon

½ cup chopped yellow onion

½ cup bacon grease

½ cup all-purpose flour

1 cup apple cider vinegar

1 cup water

1 cup sugar

¼ cup diced pimentos

1 teaspoon parsley flakes

2 teaspoons salt

1 teaspoon pepper

Place potatoes in a pot; cover with water; bring to a boil. Cook till tender; drain. Cut bacon into small pieces; cook bacon and onions till bacon is cooked and onions are tender. Add flour to the bacon mixture and grease in pan. Mix vinegar, water and sugar together; pour into flour mixture. Cook till thickens; pour over warm potatoes. Add remaining ingredients; mix well.

Restaurant Recipe

Jilly's Café & Steakhouse

1630 Gravois Road
High Ridge, MO 63049
636-449-4500
www.jillyscaféandsteakhouse.com
www.facebook/ Jilly's Café & Steakhouse

Jilly's Café & Steakhouse is a local and independently owned restaurant with romantic, friendly, and family-oriented atmospheres. With the dreams of being successful entrepreneurs and the combinations of their love for food, Joe and Dana Gisi opened the doors to Jilly's in 2006. Since the beginning, the Gisi's have wanted a place where people can feel at home while enjoying exquisite dining at reasonable prices. Enjoy great food, great friends, and great fun at Jilly's.

Monday–Sunday: 11:00 am to 11:00 pm

Jilly's Crab Encrusted Salmon

1 (8-ounce) piece skinless Norwegian salmon

Salt and pepper to taste

4 teaspoons olive oil

4 ounces lump crabmeat

2 tablespoons mayonnaise

1 teaspoon whole-grain (or coarse-ground or stone ground) mustard

3 tablespoons Japanese-style breadcrumbs (Panko)

Preheat oven to 400°. Sprinkle both sides of salmon with salt and pepper. In a skillet, over medium heat, sauté salmon 3 minutes on each side in olive oil. Remove salmon from skillet; place on a lightly greased baking pan. Using a fork, flake the crabmeat; mix with mayonnaise, mustard and Panko. Spread crab mixture on top salmon; bake uncovered for 5 minutes.

Restaurant Recipe

Jilly's Chicken Apple Wrap

1 (12-inch) tortilla wrap

4 tablespoons whipped strawberry cream cheese

2 cups fresh baby spinach

2 tablespoons toasted pecans

½ cup sliced apples

¾ cup cooked and sliced chicken breast

4 tablespoons berry poppy seed salad dressing

Spread cream cheese over favorite tortilla wrap. Toss remaining ingredients together; roll them in tortilla.

Restaurant Recipe

The Farmer's Kitchen of Hillsboro

4660 Yeager Road
Hillsboro, MO 63050
636-789-9930

The motto at The Farmers Kitchen of Hillsboro is "Just Home Cooking." They feature home-cooked breakfast, lunch, and dinner using locally sourced home-grown and farm-raised ingredients. Even though they are in a small-town country diner, you will feel right at home. They offer a wide variety of homemade desserts: pecan, apple, cherry, peach, and lemon meringue pies; cheesecakes and cupcakes; muffins; and cinnamon rolls, too. They love out-of-town visitors, so come on down.

Sunday: 8:00 am to 3:00 pm
Monday–Thursday: 6:00 am to 3:00 pm
Friday–Saturday: 6:00 am to 7:00 pm

Buffalo Chicken Soup

1 small onion, diced

2 ribs celery, chopped

¼ cup butter

¼ cup all-purpose flour

¾ cup milk

¾ cup chicken broth

2 cups diced cooked chicken

⅓ cup buffalo wing sauce

½ cup (4-ounces) processed
cheese spread

½ cup cayenne pepper

½ teaspoon celery salt

½ teaspoon garlic salt

¼ teaspoon pepper

In a 2-quart saucepan, over medium-high heat, sauté onion and celery in butter until tender. Stir in flour; slowly whisk in milk and broth. Stir in remaining ingredients; simmer over medium-low heat, stirring occasionally, until cheese is melted.

Restaurant Recipe

Blackberry French Toast

1 cup blackberry jam

1 (12-ounce) loaf French bread,
cut into ½-inch cubes

1 (8-ounce) package cream
cheese, cut into 1-inch cubes

4 large eggs

2 cups half-and-half

1 teaspoon cinnamon

1 teaspoon vanilla

½ cup firmly packed brown sugar

In a small saucepan, over medium heat, cook jam 1 to 2 minutes or until melted and smooth. Place half the bread cubes in bottom of a lightly greased 9x13-inch baking dish. Top with cream cheese cubes; drizzle with jam. Top with remaining bread cubes. Whisk together eggs, half-and-half, cinnamon and vanilla; pour over bread. Sprinkle with brown sugar. Cover tightly; chill 8 hours, or overnight. Preheat oven to 325°. Bake covered 20 minutes. Uncover and bake 10 to 15 minutes until bread is golden brown and mixture has set.

Restaurant Recipe

The Blue Owl Restaurant and Bakery

**6116 Second Street
Kimmswick, MO 63053
636-464-3128
www.theblueowl.com
Find us on Facebook**

The Blue Owl Restaurant and Bakery in Historic Kimmswick was established in August 1985 by Mary Hostetter after many prayers to make the right decision to open a restaurant and bakery in a little town, off the beaten path. The floor-length blue pinafores worn by hostesses and servers add to the ambiance and have become a signature item for The Blue Owl. Her signature dish is the levee high caramel apple pecan pie in remembrance of the flood that hit the area in '93. The levee was built and saved the town of Kimmswick. The Blue Owl has received recognition from Oprah, Paula, Jaime and Bobbie Deen, The Food Network, The Travel Channel, The Today Show, and many others.

**Tuesday–Friday: 10:00 am to 3:00 pm
Saturday–Sunday: 10:00 am to 5:00 pm**

Levee High Caramel Apple Pecan Pie

Named after the Great Flood of '93.

12 cups peeled and thinly sliced Golden Delicious Apples (16 to 18 apples)

1 cup + 1 tablespoon sugar, divided

¼ cup all-purpose flour

2 teaspoons cinnamon

Dash salt

2 deep-dish pie crusts, unbaked

1 tablespoon butter

¼ cup milk

Combine apples, 1 cup sugar, flour, cinnamon and salt. Place 2 layers apple slices in the bottom of pie crust. In a deep mixing bowl, starting from the outer edge and working your way to the middle, mound apples by hand overlapping each slice to form a tight woven web. When apples are tightly layered all the way to the top, continue to slightly round more apples over top. Holding the bottom crust in one hand, and the bowl of apples in the other hand, invert the bowl into the bottom crust. Place on counter; lift bowl away from the apples. Place butter on top of mounded apples. Cover with 2nd crust. Brush top crust with milk; sprinkle with sugar. Prick crust to allow steam to escape. Bake at 350° for 1 hour or until crust is golden brown. Remove from oven; cool before topping with Caramel Pecan Topping.

Caramel Pecan Topping

1 (21-ounce) package caramels

2 tablespoons evaporated milk

½ cup chopped pecan pieces

Melt caramels completely in microwave. Add evaporated milk; stir until smooth. Add chopped pecans; stir. Spread over cooled pie with knife, starting at the base of pie and working to the top. (Similar to icing a cake.)

Restaurant Recipe

Sym•Bowl

www.mysymbowl.com

2 locations:

11215 Manchester Road
Kirkwood, MO, 63122
314-315-4421
Monday–Friday: 9:00 am to 8:00 pm
Saturday: 10:30 am to 8:00pm

137 Chesterfield Towne Center
Chesterfield, MO 63005
636-788-0638
Monday–Friday: 10:00 am to 8:00 pm
Saturday: 10:30 am to 3:00 pm

Sym•Bowl supports you in your healthy choices and are here to make that process easier and more enjoyable for you. Sym•Bowl provides straight forward, honest, customizable food options; you are able to bring in your family and friends and feel good about your choices. Paleo, Auto-immune, Vegan, Gluten-free, they have you covered. Sym•Bowl believes in keeping the food as simple as possible. They use natural ingredients and treat them right. Because they use good, natural ingredients and utilize them with good cooking techniques they feel confident sharing with you what is in their dishes. Find your inner Flavor.

Muffins

4 cups Sunflour

1 teaspoon flax seed meal

2 tablespoons baking powder

1 teaspoon salt

2 cups applesauce

3 eggs, beaten

1 tablespoon vanilla extract

1 cup agave

In a large bowl, mix together Sunflour, flax seed meal, baking powder and salt; add applesauce, eggs, vanilla and agave. Mix well. Pour into large muffin tin. Bake at 350° for 30 minutes or until done. Yields 12 large muffins. Any combination of spices and fruit are good. Can be used to create cakes, loafs or bars.

Restaurant Recipe

Pineapple Jerk

1 cup vinegar

¾ cup water

½ whole pineapple

¼ cup agave

½ teaspoon ground ginger

¼ teaspoon ground allspice

1 teaspoon salt

Pinch thyme

1 teaspoon crushed red pepper

In a blender, process vinegar, water, pineapple and agave until smooth. Add ginger, allspice, salt, thyme and red pepper; mix well. This is a great glaze for shrimp, fish or chicken.

Restaurant Recipe

Poblano Pesto

For a light, low calorie, nutrient packed sauce with some zip, try this easy recipe. Great with pasta, chicken, or as a sauce for fish and steak.

1 bunch parsley

1 poblano pepper

1 cup fresh whole garlic

½ cup cashews

¼ cup lemon juice

1 tablespoon salt

2 cups water

In a blender, process all ingredients until smooth.

Restaurant Recipe

South 63 Café

1107 South Missouri Street
Macon, MO 63552
660-385-3201

South 63 Café may be small in appearance, but it has a big heart and a desire to feed customers not only with good food, but with laughter, teasing, wisdom, and a blessing to take you on your way. This is not your ordinary eating place in so many ways. Enjoy the best food around made with loving, caring hands. If you leave hungry, it's your fault. If you're in the neighborhood with a few minutes to spare, leave all your worries outside, come in, and make yourself at home. Wear your boots; sometimes it can get pretty deep in here. Come join the rest of the nuts inside.

Monday–Saturday: 6:00 am to 2:00 pm

Hand-Breaded Pork Tenderloin

3 eggs, beaten
2 tablespoons milk
1 sleeve saltine crackers, crushed
½ pound sliced, tenderized pork tenderloin
Oil for frying

In a bowl, combine eggs and milk. In another dish, put saltines. Dip tenderloins in egg wash then saltines, using knuckles to push pork into crumbs. Fry in skillet with oil or deep fryer 3 to 4 minutes, or until done.

Restaurant Recipe

Coconut Cream Pie

Secret recipe from Mrs. Evelyn Miles, the best pie maker around.

2 cups milk

½ stick butter

3 eggs, separated

1 cup sugar

⅓ heaping cup cornstarch

1 teaspoon vanilla

Pinch salt

1 cup shredded coconut

1 pie crust, baked

In a saucepan, heat milk and butter together. In a bowl, combine egg yolks (reserve egg whites for topping), sugar, cornstarch, vanilla and salt. Temper egg mixture with 1 cup milk mixture; add back to saucepan. Cook over low heat until thick, stirring constantly. Add coconut; stir. Pour into pie shell. Cool in refrigerator 1 hour before topping.

Topping:

3 egg whites

¼ teaspoon cream of tartar

1 teaspoon vanilla

7 teaspoons sugar

Using an electric mixer, beat egg whites until fluffy. Add cream of tartar and vanilla; beat until stiff peaks form. Gradually add sugar while beating. Spread Topping on pie; brown under broiler until golden brown.

Restaurant Recipe

Meatloaf

Made Grandma and Mama's way.

1 egg, beaten

1 teaspoon Lawry's seasoned salt

1 teaspoon pepper

1 teaspoon garlic powder

1 small onion, diced

¼ cup oatmeal

1 pound ground beef

¾ cup ketchup

In a bowl, combine egg, seasoned salt, pepper, garlic powder, onion and oatmeal; mix well. Add meat; mix. Place in a 9x9-inch casserole dish; bake at 350° for 30 minutes. Spread ketchup over top; bake another 10 minutes. Drain grease. Ready to serve.

Restaurant Recipe

Hilary's Roadhouse Diner

11488 Dorsett Road
Maryland Heights, MO 63043
314-291-0599
www.hilarysroadhousediner.com
Find us on Facebbook

Hilary was a Missouri farmer. Two of his grandsons are owner/operators in the kitchen at Hilary's Roadhouse Diner. Hilary's uses fresh-from-the-farm ingredients at the diner. The burgers are hand-pressed daily and made from pure, fresh ground beef, no additives. The sausage gravy is made fresh daily. The daily specials are created in-house using only quality ingredients. They have lots of regular customers because the locals know where the good food is. They serve breakfast all day long but close at 2 pm every day, so don't be late. Located a mile east of Highway 270 on Dorsett Road, beneath the big Verizon cell phone tower.

Monday–Saturday: 6:00 am to 2:00 pm
Sunday: 7:00 am to 2:00 pm

Hilary's Bread Pudding

1 cup sugar

1 cup light brown sugar

1 tablespoon cinnamon

1 teaspoon nutmeg

2½ cups whole milk

1 quart half-and-half

10 eggs, beaten

1 loaf Texas toast, diced
into small squares

7 tablespoons sweet butter, melted

Place bread into a buttered 9x13-inch pan. In a large mixing bowl, combine sugars, cinnamon and nutmeg; set aside. In a medium bowl, whisk milk, half-and-half, eggs and butter. Combine wet and dry ingredients, mixing thoroughly; pour over bread, making sure to cover all bread to ensure saturation before baking. Bake at 275° for 2 hours. Remove from oven; cool 30 minutes before slicing.

Restaurant Recipe

Fried Chicken Flour

1 gallon King's wheat flour

¼ pound cornstarch

½ cup garlic salt

½ cup celery salt

¼ cup onion salt

1 tablespoon black pepper

1½ tablespoons iodized salt

½ tablespoon white pepper

¼ cup dried rubbed sage

½ tablespoon ground thyme

Mix all ingredients in a large bowl and store in an airtight container.

Restaurant Recipe

Harmony Café & Coffee Shop

204 South Main Street
Monroe City, MO 63456
573-735-2022
www.facebook.com/Harmony-Café-Coffee-Shop

Sarah and Mandi opened Harmony on pure faith and they welcome you to come sit, visit, and enjoy home-cooked food in a loving atmosphere to feed your body and soul. Whether you're a local regular or just passing through town, their mission is for you to come in and make yourself at home. Enjoy a game of checkers, shopping, lounge in the sitting area, or dine at the tables or bar. At this unique establishment, you will find a restored historic building that serves homemade soups, paninis, salads, and desserts. There also is a complete coffee bar with many flavors including frozen, hot, and cold coffees to choose from.

Monday–Friday: 8:00 am to 5:00 pm
Saturday: 8:00 am to 3:00 pm
Closed on Mondays through the winter

Chicken Salad

2 boneless chicken breasts, boiled and shredded

1 cup quartered seedless grapes

1 cup chopped celery

¼ cup sunflower seeds

½ to 1 cup mayonnaise

Salt and pepper to taste

Combine all ingredients. Cover; refrigerate overnight. Serve with crackers, on bread or in a wrap next day.

Restaurant Recipe

Banana Cream Pie

Crust:

1 cup all-purpose flour

1 cup crushed pecans

1 stick butter, softened

Combine all ingredients; press in bottom of a pie pan. Bake at 350° for 15 minutes or until golden brown. Cool.

First Layer:

1 (8-ounce) package cream cheese, softened

1 cup homemade whipped cream

1 cup powdered sugar

Combine all ingredients in mixing bowl; mix on low speed for 1 minute. Increase to medium speed for 3 minutes or until creamy; set aside.

Second Layer:

3 bananas, sliced

Third Layer:

1 (5.1-ounce) box vanilla instant pudding, prepared

Fourth Layer:

2 cups homemade whipped cream

1 to 2 tablespoons chopped pecans

Pour First Layer in cooled Crust; top with remaining layers in order, ending with chopped pecans.

Coleslaw

1 package colorful coleslaw mix

½ cup mayonnaise

2 tablespoons milk

1 tablespoon lemon juice

2 tablespoons sugar

1 (11-ounce) can Mandarin orange slices, drained

¼ cup craisins

Place coleslaw mix in a bowl; set aside. In another bowl, mix remaining ingredients; pour over slaw, mixing well. Cover and refrigerate or serve immediately.

Restaurant Recipe

Boots Bar and Grill

409 Booneslick Road
New Florence, MO 63363
855-388-1672
www.bootsbarandgrill.net

Boot's Bar & Grill is the place to go for delicious made-from-scratch dishes that you will enjoy while watching the big game. The menu features tasty grilled tenderloin, half-pound burgers and more. There are also daily lunch specials Boots is a true bar and grill, with three big-screen TVs, making it great for families or for a game-day gathering. They also offer the coldest beer in town. The menu features homemade dishes made fresh using family recipes and the finest ingredients available served by a friendly staff with years of restaurant experience.

Monday–Thursday; 11:00 am to 11:00 pm
Friday & Saturday: 11:00 am to 1:30 am
Sunday: 11:00 am to midnight

Bacon-Spinach Muffins

2 eggs

⅓ cup butter, melted

½ cup milk

1½ cups all-purpose flour

2 tablespoons sugar

2 teaspoons baking powder

¼ teaspoon salt

⅛ teaspoon freshly ground pepper

1½ cups fresh baby spinach,
coarsely chopped

12 slices bacon, cooked and crumbled

½ cup shredded Swiss cheese

Heat oven to 400°. Spray 2 (6-cup) muffin pans with nonstick spray. In a large bowl, beat eggs, butter and milk until well blended. In a second bowl, combine flour, sugar, baking powder, salt and pepper; stir. Combine mixtures with a spoon just until dry ingredients are moistened. Stir in spinach, bacon and cheese. Divide batter evenly among muffin cups, filling each about three-fourths full. Bake about 20 minutes or until toothpick inserted in center comes out clean. Remove muffins from pan to cooling rack; cool 5 minutes. Serve warm.

Local Favorite

Curried Fruit Bake

1 (15-ounce) can mixed fruit
(large pieces), drained

2 slices pineapple

¼ stick butter, melted

¼ cup brown sugar

½ teaspoon curry powder

½ cup pecan halves

Arrange fruits in a 9x9-inch casserole dish; pour melted butter over fruit. Mix sugar and curry together; sprinkle over fruit. Top with pecans; bake at 350° for 45 minutes. Serves 4.

Local Favorite

NATURAL WONDER, FAMOUS LITERARY LOCATION, OR MAUSOLEUM FOR MAD-DOCTOR EXPERIMENTS?

Mark Twain Cave, Hannibal

Mark Twain Cave, located near Hannibal, is the oldest operating show cave in the state, giving tours continuously since 1886. It became a registered National Natural Landmark in 1972. Serving as inspiration for McDougal's Cave in the novel *The Adventures of Tom Sawyer* by Mark Twain, the cave was later renamed in honor of the author, a Hannibal native. Mark Twain actually wrote about the cave in five of his books, bringing thousands of people from all over the world to Hannibal by steamboat to see this cave that they had read about.

Before it was known as Mark Twain Cave, the cave was purchased in 1848 by Dr. Joseph Nash McDowell and was used for several years as a laboratory for his experiments on human corpses. His most notable experiment involved placing his deceased 14-year old daughter, who died of pneumonia, in a glass and copper cylinder coffin filled with alcohol that was suspended from the cave by chains. After two years, the experiment proved a failure and the girl's body was forcibly removed by angry Hannibal citizens who learned about it from children who discovered it while exploring the cave. Many townsfolk believed Dr. McDowell used bodies stolen from area graves for other experiments.

In 1879, Jesse James used Mark Twain Cave as a hide-out after robbing a bank in Saverton, Missouri. His signature can still be seen in the cave today. And President Jimmy Carter and the First Family visited the cave on August 23, 1979, and signed its guest book, which is still displayed in the gift shop.

The cave is always around 52 degrees and while it is not exceptional in size or formations, it is a fun and fascinating labyrinth of twisty passages. Special alcoves and hallways are given nicknames, based on their appearance, the shape of the outcrops, or historical events—The Alligator, Mother Hubbard's Cupboard, Marriage Corner, Aladdin's Palace, and the Waterfall are a few favorites.

Mark Twain Cave has been explored by locals since its discovery in the 1800's. Since becoming a tourist attraction in 1886, it has been shown continuously, including throughout both World Wars and the Great Depression. And still today, the cave is a fun experience for cave lovers, Mark Twain enthusiasts, and history buffs.

In one spot of the cave, there are hundreds of signatures dated for a period of well over 100 years. The limestone has been estimated by geologists as around 350 million years old. The cave passages were formed about 100 million years ago. Mark Twain Cave covers six and a half miles consisting of four entrances and 260 passages. The cave maintains a year around temperature of 52 degrees.

Mark Twain Cave
300 Cave Hollow Road
Hannibal, MO 63401
573-221-1656
www.marktwaincave.com

The Junction Restaurant and Lounge

28840 State Highway 19
Perry, MO 63462
573-565-3620
www.thejunctionmo.com
"A Tradition at Mark Twain Lake"

The Junction has been around since 1983, and chances are, you or someone you've met can tell you a great memory from "when they were younger" at The Junction. This is a place where tradition and the hometown feel are ever present. What once started as a small restaurant, where the bait shop is currently located, has now grown and expanded into what you see today. The restaurant offers a variety of food, drinks and accommodations for every family member. The Junction caters to the local population and welcomes seasonal visitors during fishing, hunting, and family vacations. They offer home-style, affordable lunch specials, tempting nightly dinner specials, and a menu with a wide array of selections.

Sunday–Thursday: 6:00 am to 8:30 pm
Friday & Saturday: 6:00 am to 9:00 pm
Check Facebook for current hours.

Breaded Pork Tenderloin

1 sleeve saltine crackers, divided

2 large eggs

1 cup milk

Salt and pepper to taste

4 (6-to 8-ounce) boneless
tenderized pork chops

4 buns, toasted

In a food processor, pulse half the crackers to make cracker meal. Crush other half; mix together to make cracker breading. Set aside. Beat eggs, milk, salt and pepper together; set aside. Dip pork in egg mixture; place on top of cracker breading. Cover pork with breading, gently pushing breading into pork to help stick. Deep fry at 325° for 7 to 9 minutes until floating and golden brown; drain. Place on buns; top with your favorite veggies and condiments.

Restaurant Recipe

Chicken Picatta

2½ cups flour

2 tablespoons chopped parsley

Salt and pepper, to taste

Oil (enough to fry chicken)

4 boneless chicken breasts

1½ cups butter

2 lemons, juiced

2 tablespoons white wine

¼ cup capers

Lemon wedge, for garnish

Mix together flour, parsley, salt and pepper; set aside. In a skillet, heat enough oil to cover chicken halfway over medium-high heat. Dredge chicken in flour mixture; cook 6 to 7 minutes per side, being careful to not burn. Remove from heat; drain. In a saucepan over low heat, melt butter; add lemon juice and wine. Cook 5 minutes. Add capers; cook 1 minute more. Pour sauce over chicken; garnish with lemon wedge.

Restaurant Recipe

Hackers Restaurant

106 North Jackson Street
Shelbyville, MO 63469
573-633-2114
www.hackersrestaurant.com

Hackers opened their doors in August 2014 with a three-point goal—great food, good service, and a warm friendly décor. They have met those goals and much more. Chef B has developed a bread pudding that keeps you coming back for more. His pastas are made fresh with each order as well as everything else on the menu. Check out the open kitchen as Chef B prepares your food. There is a fully stocked bar that includes beer, mixed drinks, and an assortment of wines. Hackers aims to please you from your appetizer to dessert.

Lunch: Monday–Friday: 11:00 am to 1:30 pm
Dinner: Tuesday–Saturday: 5:00 pm to Close

Bread Pudding

2 red apples, cored, peeled, thinly sliced

1 teaspoon cinnamon

1 cup water

1 pint heavy cream

1 (8-ounce) package white chocolate chips

1 tablespoon vanilla

12 croissants, torn into bite-size pieces

Tempura Batter (see recipe below)

White chocolate sauce

Caramel sauce

In a pan over medium heat, cook apples with cinnamon and water until tender; set aside. Bring heavy cream to a slight boil; add white chocolate chips. Whisk until blended; add vanilla. In a large bowl, add croissants, apples with juice and heavy cream mixture. Stir well. Spray ramekins with baking spray; fill with mixture. Bake at 350° for 1 hour. Cool and cut into 4 pieces. Roll in Tempura Batter; fry for 5 minutes or until golden brown. Drizzle with white chocolate and caramel sauces. Serve.

Tempura Batter:

1 cup all-purpose flour

¼ teaspoon cinnamon

¼ cup water

Mix to a pancake-like thickness. Ready for dipping.

Restaurant Recipe

Shrimp and Clam Linguine

12 fresh shrimp

4 ounces chopped clams

¼ cup thinly sliced onion

2 tablespoons vegetable oil

1 (7-ounce) package linguine noodles, cooked, drained

½ cup heavy cream

3 tablespoons grated Parmesan cheese

2 tablespoons chopped fresh parsley and oregano

Sauté shrimp, clams and onions in hot oil for 3 to 4 minutes. Add noodles and heavy cream; bring to a boil. Add Parmesan cheese; cook to thicken. Garnish with fresh herbs. Serve with grilled baguette bread.

Restaurant Recipe

Gibby's

9A Paul Parks Drive
St. Clair, MO 63077
636-629-3636

If you are looking for a place to eat good food and have a great time in a casual atmosphere, Gibby's is the place for you. Gibby's, named after the owner's Grandfather, is the place to go for the best in pizzas, salads, homemade pasta, wings and burgers. There is something to please everyone in your group. Good food served by friendly staff, what more could you want? Try the locally famous Great Gibby Burger a three pound giant burger; if you eat it all, your picture will be added to the wall of fame. Gibby's is conveniently located on the famous Route 66.

Sunday–Thursday: 10:30 am to 10:00 pm
Friday & Saturday: 10:30 am to Midnight

Pasta Con Broccoli

1 cup broccoli crowns
⅛ cup fresh mushrooms
2 cups prepared penne pasta
1 cup half-and-half
Salt and pepper to taste
⅛ teaspoon granulated garlic
2 ounces prepared meat sauce
2 ounces shredded provolone cheese
1 ounce shredded Parmesan cheese

In a 10-inch skillet, combine all ingredients except cheeses. Bring to rolling boil; add cheeses. Stir until cheese thickens to desired consistency (may use little more cheese). Serve and enjoy.

Restaurant Recipe

Tornado Burger

½ pound ^{9}⁰⁄₁₀ ground beef
Salt and pepper to taste
Minced garlic to taste
Steak sauce
8 to 10 slices jalapeño peppers
Provolone cheese slice
Hoagie buns, toasted
Onion rings

Form beef into patty; cook on charbroiler to desired doneness. Turn burger once; add steak sauce, jalapeno and cheese. Remove from heat; place on bun with a few onion rings.

Restaurant Recipe

Mama Campisi's "On the Hill"

2132 Edwards Street
St. Louis, MO 63110
314-776-3100
Find us on Facebook

Mama Campisi's, a longtime staple on "The Hill," specializes in southern, Italian-style cuisine. Mama's menu has something for every palate, even offering vegan and gluten-free pastas. Mama's is the home of the toasted ravioli. Mickey Garagiola was a busboy here when the fortunate accident happened. It turned out to be the most popular item on the menu. However, Mama's offers many other delicious items—Chicken Spedini and homemade Lasagna are just a couple. Mama's offers culinary classes and wine dinners. They have a beautiful banquet facility with private entrance, bar, and restrooms. Mama's offers off-site catering for any size group.

Sunday–Thursday: 11:00 am to 9:00 pm
Friday & Saturday: 11:00 am to 10:00 pm
Twitter-Instagram-Snapchat-Pinterest

Cannoli

4 cups whole milk ricotta cheese

1½ cups powdered sugar,
plus more for garnish

2 ounces amaretto liqueur

1 tablespoon vanilla extract

¼ cup semisweet mini chocolate chips

Cherries

Whipped cream

Shaved chocolate

Cannoli shells

Drain ricotta cheese over cheesecloth if ricotta is watery. Combine ricotta cheese, powdered sugar, liqueur and vanilla extract until combined. Fold chocolate chips into ricotta mixture, being careful not to overmix. (For a lighter filling, you may whip 1 cup heavy whipping cream to form stiff peaks, and fold into filling mixture.) Chill filling 30 minutes before piping into cannoli shells. Garnish by sprinkling powdered sugar on top. Cut a cherry into 2 pieces, placing a piece on each end. Whipped cream, a cherry, and shaved chocolate can also be used to garnish the top. Keep refrigerated until time of serving.

Restaurant Recipe

Stacked STL

7637 Ivory Street
St. Louis, MO 63111
314-544-4900
www.StackedSTL.com

With the idea to allow people a little more creativity with building their own burgers, Chef Laura, fiancé Matt, and best friend, Sam's idea soon snowballed into the now-famous Stacked Burger Bar. Walking into the restaurant you are greeted with bright colors, an eclectic array of knick-knacks, and that signature orange cow. Once seated, choose between one of the 13 (and growing) signature burgers Chef Laura has created, or grab that pencil and sushi-style pad of paper and start creating your own. With over 70 options available, they offer a turkey patty, black bean burger, locally raised grass-fed beef, and so on. Everything is made in-house with as many fresh local ingredients as possible, to give you the best building blocks for your perfect burger masterpiece.

Monday–Thursday: 11:00 am to 9:30 pm
Friday & Saturday: 11:00 am to 10:00 pm
Sunday: 11:00 am to 9:00 pm

Strawberry Maple Jam

**5 pounds fresh strawberries,
hulled and quartered**

2 cups sugar

2 cups maple syrup

1 medium-sized orange, zested

In a large non-reactive pot, add strawberries and sugar; stir to coat. Cover; let sit a few hours until the juices have started to come out. Cook over low heat until strawberries begin to break down and syrup has thickened. Stir in maple syrup; allow to thicken a little more. (You are looking for a spreadable consistency.) Remove from heat; add orange zest and stir. If you plan to use the jam within the week, just store in airtight jars. If storing longer, follow proper canning guidelines to preserve. Yields 2 quarts.

Restaurant Recipe

BBQ Sauce

1 chipotle, chopped

2 teaspoons adobo sauce

2 cups pineapple juice, divided

7 cups ketchup

2 cups water

1 tablespoon liquid smoke

3 tablespoons molasses

Blend chipotle and adobo with 1 cup pineapple juice until smooth. In a pot, combine all the ingredients, including the chipotle mixture. (For a sweeter sauce, leave out the chipotle and adobo.) Cook over low heat for an hour or so, stirring occasionally, until thickened and darker in color. Store in an airtight jar or container. Use on grilled pork, beef or chicken. Yields 2 quarts.

Restaurant Recipe

WORLD'S LARGEST UNDERPANTS (AND MORE!)

City Museum, St. Louis

Is it a museum or a playground? Who cares what you call it, because it's super fun for visitors of all ages. City Museum features precarious places to climb and secret chutes for sliding as well as exhibits on the architecture of St. Louis.

If all that's not enough, the museum features the World's Largest Underpants, the World's Largest Pencil, Elvis Presley's travel trailer, and a rooftop Ferris wheel. At first glance, you will know immediately that St. Louis City Museum is an outstanding place for families. It is also terrific for date night or adults-only trips. On Friday and Saturday nights, it stays open late so adults can freely play and run around without worrying about trampling a small child.

The 600,000-square-foot building, formerly home to the International Shoe Factory, was purchased in 1995 by Bob Cassilly. The classically-trained sculptor set out to make a funhouse for young and old out of unique, reclaimed objects found within the city's municipal borders.

One space is a series of tunnels underneath the building, a giant indoor treehouse, and a slide that goes into the museum's pump room. The collection includes cranes, old bridges, a human-sized hamster wheel, vintage opera posters, a room of preserved insects, a bank vault, a fish tank full of turtles (and one very friendly 39-pound catfish), and at least one alien dressed like Elvis in a coffin—all accessible via stairs, elevator, tunnel, or slide.

One of the coolest and most entertaining tourist places around, the space is always growing and changing.

City Museum
750 North 16th Street
St. Louis, MO 63103
314-231-2489
www.citymuseum.org

FUN FACTS:

- Two planes were purchased after the flood of 1993, and now, the planes are part of the museum's MonstroCity; visitors can crawl through a series of wire tubes and explore the interior of the planes.

- Big Eli is a 30-foot-high Ferris wheel, which was manufactured in 1940 and was found in a barn. After being fully restored, Big Eli found a home on the roof, giving visitors a spectacular view of the city.

- The World's Largest Pencil is 76 feet long and weighs 21,500 pounds. It contains 4,000 pounds of graphite and is the equivalent of 1,900,000 regular pencils.

- The Largest Pair of Underpants once went missing from the museum's walls. They mysteriously reappeared 3.5 weeks later.

- There is a large cross on the wall taken from the east wing of the Alexian Brothers Hospital in St. Louis. That's where the 1940's exorcism that inspired the novel and film *The Exorcist* took place.

Tony's

410 Market Street
St. Louis, MO 63102
314-231-7007
www.tonysstlouis.com
Find us on Facebook

As it's been for over half a century, when most people are asked to name the truly greatest restaurants of St Louis, Tony's is most always, and justifiably, at the very top of the list. It's the special place for special occasions or to make any occasion extra special. The prime, corn-fed steaks are hand-cut, sauces start simmering at 6 or 7 a.m., fresh fish from the cold Atlantic is flown in 2 to 3 times a week and Dover sole arrives by air from Europe weekly—even the herbs are fresh. The soup course might include pheasant consomme or a rich cream concoction, the salads are sensational and the extensive list of appetizers can easily be a substitute for an entrée.

Tuesday–Thursday: 5:30 pm to 9:30 pm
Friday & Saturday; 5:00 pm to 10:00 pm

Pan-Roasted Quail

12 quail

12 thin slices pancetta

12 fresh or dried sage leaves

3 tablespoons butter

2 tablespoons olive oil

Salt

Black pepper in grinder

½ cup dry white wine

Thoroughly wash quail inside and out under cold running water; drain in colander 20 minutes. Pat quail dry; stuff each cavity with 1 slice pancetta and 1 sage leaf. In a lidded sauté pan that will accommodate all the quail without overlapping, heat butter and oil on high heat. Add quail, turning and browning quail on all sides. Sprinkle with salt and pepper; add wine, turning the bird 1 time to coat. Allow wine to cook 1 minute. Lower heat to medium; cover pan with lid leaving slightly askew. Cook 45 minutes or until quail feels tender and meat pulls away from bone easily. Check to make sure there is sufficient juice in pan to keep quail from sticking, may add water 1 to 2 tablespoons at a time. Remove quail from pan; add ¼ cup water to pan; raise heat to high, loosen residues from bottom of pan. Allow all water to boil away; pour pan juices over quail; serve immediately.

Restaurant Recipe

Pasta, Clams, Shrimp

3 tablespoons extra virgin olive oil

3 garlic cloves, chopped

2¼ ponds clams, washed

⅔ cup white wine

1 (16-ounce) package
pasta, your choice

1 pound shelled shrimp

1 fresh red chili, seeded and chopped

4 ounces arugula leaves

In a large, thick-bottomed pan with a lid, add olive oil and garlic; cook until garlic softens. Add clams and wine; cover, cooking until clams are opened, about 2 minutes (discard any that remain closed). Add shrimp, arugula and chili; cover again to wilt arugula. Keep warm. Cook pasta in boiling salted water until al dente; drain. Add clams; heat for 1 minute. Season and drizzle with olive oil.

Restaurant Recipe

Vernon's BBQ and Catering

6707 Vernon Avenue
St. Louis, MO 63130
314-726-1227
vernonsbbq.com
Find us on Facebook

Come in to Vernon's BBQ and enjoy some of the best barbecue ever to be eaten. Don't expect just smoked meats—although he does the best brisket, pork, ham, turkey, and chicken; they do tofu, too. Seems like Vernon can smoke anything that comes through the door. He even does seasonal smoked fruit. Now that is what I call a variety to please the taste buds. Don't forget the sides—tequila lime green beans, potato salad, mac-n-cheese, corn with peppers, and Matt's secret cornbread. Cover the 'que with any of the five flavorful sauces—from Peachy Keen to Little Smokey, you will find one to suit your taste.

Sunday & Tuesday–Thursday: 11:00 am to 9:00 pm
Friday & Saturday: 11:00 am to 10:00 pm

Smoked Peaches

Per Serving:

**1 fresh ripe peaches, cut in
half and remove pit**

½ teaspoon butter

1 tablespoon brown sugar

½ teaspoon cinnamon

Fire up the grill; create a medium-sized,
indirect-heat fire. Lay peaches skin-side
down; place ½ teaspoon butter where
pit was. Put 1 tablespoon brown sugar
on top of butter; sprinkle ½ teaspoon
cinnamon over open face of peach. Add
your favorite smoking wood to the fire at
this time; grill 10 to 15 minutes, peach
will get soft inside the skin. Enjoy.

Restaurant Recipe

Tequila Lime Green Beans

2 tablespoons toasted sesame oil

**2 quarts fresh green beans,
stemmed and rinsed**

Kosher salt, to taste

Ground black pepper to taste

4 tablespoons tequila, heated

3 to 4 fresh limes

In a Wok or large sauté pan over high
heat, heat oil until smoke starts to
appear; toss in beans. Sprinkle salt and
pepper over top; toss to evenly season
beans. Keeping beans evenly spread on
cooking surface, cook until beans are
hot and char marks start to appear. Add
tequila; hot spoon tequila over beans
tossing to evenly distribute. (Keeping
heat on allows alcohol to burn off,
leaving tequila flavoring.) Turn heat off;
squeeze 3 to 4 fresh limes (depending on
size) over beans and toss to finish. Enjoy.

Restaurant Recipe

The Vine Café

3171 South Grand
St. Louis, MO 63118
314-776-0991
www.thevinestl.com

The Vine is a traditional Lebanese restaurant where they take pride in authentic flavors. The menu is created from family recipes served for generations. It is their goal to bring the comfort and spirit of the Mediterranean to St. Louis. Whether it's freshly baked pita bread or the daily selection of sweets, every dish from the kitchen carries the love of a home-cooked meal, served in cozy digs with a hookah lounge and small grocery.

Monday–Saturday: 11:00 am to 9:00 pm
Sunday: 11:00 am to 10:00 pm

Garlic Sauce

1 head garlic, peeled
1 tablespoon sea salt
1 cup mayonnaise
½ cup fresh lemon juice
2 tablespoons olive oil

Place all ingredients in a blender; blend until smooth. Use as a dip or sauce for anything. This is even great as a dip for French fries.

Restaurant Recipe

Batata Harra

4 large potatoes, cut into ¾-inch cubes

Oil for frying

Salt to taste

3 tablespoons olive oil

5 to 8 large fresh garlic cloves, crushed

1 bunch green cilantro, remove stems and rough chop (or ½ cup dried cilantro leaves)

1 tablespoon crushed red pepper

1 lemon, juiced

In a skillet, fry potatoes in oil until golden crispy; lightly salt. In a deep frying pan, heat 3 tablespoons olive oil over medium heat; add crushed garlic. Do not brown; it should remain slightly raw. Add a dash of salt, cilantro, crushed red pepper and lemon juice; sauté 2 minutes, stirring occasionally. Mix in fried potatoes; cook 3 to 5 more minutes while gently stirring. Plate and sprinkle with additional chopped cilantro.

Restaurant Recipe

Hummus

1 (15-ounce) can garbanzo beans (chickpeas), drained

4 tablespoons tahini

2 tablespoons extra virgin olive oil, plus extra for garnish

1½ tablespoons fresh lemon juice

¼ cup water

3 cloves garlic, crushed

½ teaspoon ground cumin

1 pinch paprika

Blend all ingredients, except paprika, in food processor until smooth, for approximately 1 minute. Use spatula to scoop into a bowl; dust with paprika. Drizzle additional olive oil over top before serving. Serve with pita bread or chips.

Restaurant Recipe

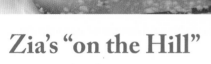

Zia's "on the Hill"

5256 Wilson Avenue
St Louis, MO 63110
314-776-0020
www.zias.com

Zia's restaurant was established in 1985 by brothers Dennis and Angelo Chiodini. Zia's means "aunt" in Italian and it was named this after Dennis and Angelo's two aunts who came from Italy. With their recipes, the brothers grew the business from a small sandwich shop to what it is now, a full-service restaurant that seats over 150 guests. Zia's serves traditional northern Italian cuisine, specializing in pasta, chicken, and steak.

Monday–Saturday: 11:00 am to 10:00 pm

Beef Sotto

2 (8-ounce) center-cut beef filets

1 tablespoon minced garlic

1 teaspoon cracked black pepper

1 cup sliced fresh mushrooms

**2 cups Zia's White Wine
Lemon Butter Sauce**

Preheat grill on medium-high heat. Cook steaks to liking, approximately 7 minutes on each side to prepare to a medium temperature. In a medium saucepan, sauté garlic and pepper; add mushrooms and white wine sauce; bring to a simmer. Cook until mushrooms are tender. Pour prepared sauce over cooked beef and enjoy.

Restaurant Recipe

Chicken Spiedini Proscuitto

**2 pounds chicken tenders,
cut into bite-sized pieces**

1 cup Zia's Sweet Italian Salad Dressing

1 cup Italian-seasoned breadcrumbs

**3 cups Zia's White Wine
Lemon Butter sauce**

1 cup fresh sliced mushrooms

1 cup diced prosciutto ham

1 cup shredded Provel cheese

Combine chicken and salad dressing in a zip-close bag; marinate 1½ hours. Discard marinade. Toss chicken in breadcrumbs; skewer 8 ounces on each skewer. Grill over medium heat until juices run clear, approximately 12 minutes. Bring Zia's wine sauce to a simmer over low heat. Add mushrooms and prosciutto. Cook until mushrooms are tender. Remove chicken from skewers to a serving plate. Top with cheese and sauce, then garnish with additional cheese. (May prepare in the oven at 350°. Do not use skewers; instead arrange in oven-safe dish and bake approximately 20 minutes.)

Restaurant Recipe

Troy Mediterranean Cuisine

19 Stonegate Shopping Center Suite19
Valley Park, MO 63088
636-517-1141
troymediterranean.com

Troy Mediterranean Cuisine is the hottest new Mediterranean restaurant in town. The owner/head chef has more than 15 years experience and a true passion for Mediterranean flavors. This passion comes through in the tasty, high-quality cuisine coming from the kitchen. It extends far beyond baklava and gyros; it stretches from salads to sandwiches and large plates. Walk in and your stomach will start growling, letting you know you are in the best place in town to eat. Carry out, dine-in, and catering are all available. They even offer discounts for large groups. A great place for family and friends to meet and eat.

Monday–Thursday: 11:00 am to 9:00 pm
Friday & Saturday: 11:00 am to 11:00 pm
Sunday: 12:00 pm to 8:00 pm

Kebab Salad

2 eggplant slices, grilled
2 yellow bell pepper slices, grilled
2 red bell pepper slices, grilled
Salad greens (one serving)
Salt to taste
Pepper to taste
1 clove garlic, smashed
2 teaspoons olive oil
1 tablespoon vinegar

After grilling vegetables, cut to finger size. In a bowl, mix together, eggplant, peppers, salad greens, salt, pepper, garlic, olive oil and vinegar. Plate; ready to eat.

Restaurant Recipe

Central REGION

The Iron Horse Hotel and Restaurant

101 Main Street
Blackwater, MO 65322
660-846-2011
www.ironhorsehotel.com
Find us on Facebook

The Iron Horse Hotel and Restaurant offers a "taste of life from days gone by," reflecting the glory days of the railroad barons, boasting ornate wood, iron craftsmanship, period furnishings, inviting parlor, elegant staircases, and courtyard gardens. The restaurant features both casual and fine dining in one of two intimate dining rooms. Diners feast on Creole classics like Fried Green Tomatoes and Shrimp, Blackened Pork Chops with Red Beans and Rice, Mediterranean-Style Fish, Italian Pastas, and traditional Southern classics. The signature dessert, Snickers à la Minnie, was created to honor Blackwater resident, Minnie Morgan, credited for naming the beloved Snickers Bar. Available for private functions.

Hotel open 7 days a week
Restaurant Seasonal: Call for hours
Beginning March or April
Lunch on weekends: 12:00 pm to 2:00 pm
Dinner: Friday & Saturday: 5:30 pm to 8:00 pm

Banana Foster Cheesecake

¼ cup butter

1 cup dark brown sugar

½ teaspoon cinnamon

¼ cup banana liqueur

¼ cup dark rum

3 to 4 bananas

Cheesecake slices

Powdered sugar

Over medium-high heat, melt butter. Add sugar and cinnamon; cook until sugar begins to dissolve. Stir in liqueur, reduce by ⅓. Remove pan from heat; add rum. Return to heat and flambe till alcohol burns off. Slice bananas into pan; toss to heat through. Pour over cheesecake slices; dust with powdered sugar.

Restaurant Recipe

Sweet and Spicy Coleslaw

Served daily with lunch sandwiches.

2 (1-pound) bags shredded slaw mix

1 small yellow onion, shredded

½ cup mayonnaise

¼ cup Dijon mustard

2 teaspoons apple cider vinegar

1 cup sugar

1 teaspoon black pepper

½ teaspoon cayenne pepper

Pinch kosher salt

In a large container, combine slaw mix and onion. In another bowl, whisk together mayonnaise, mustard, vinegar, sugar, black pepper, cayenne pepper and salt. Toss dressing with the slaw mixture; add more salt and freshly ground pepper to taste. Cover; chill 1 hour before serving.

Restaurant Recipe

WHERE CLYDESDALES ARE BORN

Warm Springs Ranch, Booneville

Have you ever wondered where Clydesdales get their start before they pull beer wagons and make commercials? Warm Springs Ranch is a 300-acre Anheuser-Busch Clydesdale breeding facility and home to more than 100 Clydesdales.

It all started in the mid-1800's when large numbers of German immigrants arrived to St. Louis, mainly due to political upheavals in Germany and Bohemia in 1848. Soon the principal industry in the area was brewing beer, and the immigrants introduced Lager-style beer to the United States. Eberhard Anheuser was part owner of a brewery, and Adolphus Busch had a partnership in a brewing supply business. The two met and in 1861, Adolphus Busch and Lilly Anheuser were married. Adolphus worked for his father-in-law and later became a partner when he purchased half ownership in the brewery. Adolphus Busch died in 1913 and was succeeded by his son, August A. Busch Sr.

Then on April 7, 1933, Augustus, Sr.'s two sons, August A. Busch, Jr. and Adolphus Busch III, surprised their father with the gift of a six-horse Clydesdale hitch to commemorate the repeal of Prohibition. Realizing the marketing potential of a horse-drawn beer wagon, the company also arranged to have a second six-horse Clydesdale hitch sent to New York on April 7th to mark the event. The Clydesdales drew a crowd of thousands as they clattered down the streets of New York City to the Empire State Building.

Shortly after the hitch was introduced, the six-horse Clydesdale team was increased to eight. On March 30, 1950, in commemoration of the opening of the Newark Brewery, a Dalmatian was introduced as the Budweiser Clydesdales' mascot. Now, a Dalmatian travels with each of the Clydesdale hitches. Today, Anheuser-Busch owns approximately 250 Clydesdales; they continue to be an enduring symbol of the brewer's heritage, tradition, and commitment to quality.

Warm Springs Ranch
25270 Highway 98
Booneville, MO 25270
www.warmspringsranch.com

FUN FACTS:

- In the early 19th century, farmers living along the banks of the River Clyde in Lanarkshire, Scotland, imported a few Great Flemish Horses and mated them with local mares. This was the birth of the Clydesdale.

- Each hitch horse consumes as much as 20 to 25 quarts of whole grains, minerals, and vitamins, 50 to 60 pounds of hay, and 30 gallons of water per day.

- The official home of the Budweiser Clydesdales is an ornate brick and stained-glass stable built in 1885 on the historic 100-acre Anheuser-Busch Brewery complex in St. Louis.

WARM SPRINGS RANCH
HOME OF THE WORLD-FAMOUS
Budweiser Clydesdales

L.A. Cafe

525 Ozark Avenue
Cabool, MO 65689
417-962-2700
www.facebook.com/LA-Café

L.A. Cafe is just a small café but growing bigger in size and in the hearts of their customers. This small-town, family-operated business is doing what they can and striving for customer satisfaction all while living the dream of owning their own family business. Besides their food, the best thing about the small-town atmosphere is the family feel the customers receive on a daily basis. Warm smiles and hot food are served daily at the L.A. Café.

Monday–Saturday: 5:00 am to 2:00 pm
Sunday: 6:00 am to 2:00 pm

Blue Cheese Dressing

10 cups mayonnaise

5 cups sour cream

½ cup vinegar

½ cup oil

5 teaspoons garlic salt

2½ teaspoons black pepper

1 pound blue cheese crumbles

Using an electric mixer, combine mayonnaise, sour cream, vinegar, oil, garlic salt and pepper; mix well. Fold in crumbles.

Restaurant Recipe

Buttermilk Biscuits

2 cups all-purpose flour

2½ teaspoons baking powder

½ teaspoon baking soda

Dash salt

1 tablespoon sugar

½ cup butter

¾ cup buttermilk

In a bowl, combine dry ingredients; cut butter into flour mixture. Add buttermilk; mix just until combined. Pat out dough on floured surface to ½-inch thickness; cut out biscuits. Place on greased pan; bake at 450° for 10 to 15 minutes or until golden brown. Makes 6 biscuits.

Restaurant Recipe

Bread Pudding

2 eggs, beaten

2 cups milk

1 cup sugar

1 tablespoon melted butter

1 teaspoon cinnamon

10 bread slices, cubed

In a bowl, combine eggs, milk, sugar , butter and cinnamon; mix well. Add bread; refrigerate overnight. Pour into a 9x13-inch casserole dish; bake at 350° for 60 minutes.

Custard Sauce:

⅔ cup sugar

2 tablespoons flour

1 cup water

8 tablespoons real butter

1 teaspoon vanilla

In a saucepan, cook sugar, flour and water over medium heat until thickened. Remove from heat; add butter and vanilla. Mix well to combine; pour over bread pudding.

Restaurant Recipe

What's yo mama cookin' today?

BURGERS' SMOKEHOUSE

SIMPLE TRADITIONS SINCE 1952

Burgers' Smokehouse

32819 Highway 87 South
California, MO 65018
800-624-5426
www.smokehouse.com
www.facebook.com/burgerssmokehouse

Situated in the heart of the Ozarks, Burgers' Smokehouse offers customers a taste of the old combined with the new. From the unique visitors center to their sandwich bar and company store, they offer something for everyone. Come by and learn more about the history and try some country cured and smoked ham or turkey. Don't forget to pick up a package of bacon or sausage to enjoy later. The Burgers' Smokehouse family looks forward to having you as their guest.

Open Year Round: Monday–Friday: 8:00 am to 5:00 pm
October–December: Open Saturdays 8:00 am to 5:00 pm

Country Ham with Red Eye Gravy

Burgers' Country Ham Slices

2 tablespoons oil or bacon grease for frying

½ cup brewed coffee

Heat skillet to 350° on medium heat; add oil. Sear ham slices 2 minutes each side. (Hint: cover skillet during frying to tenderize and seal in flavor.) Remove ham; pour off excess grease. Add coffee or ½ cup water, depending on your taste, to skillet; stir to release drippings. Cook until reduced by half; Pour gravy over ham, eggs or biscuits.

Family Favorite

Country Ham Breakfast Casserole

¼ cup butter

1 cup unseasoned croutons

½ cup shredded Cheddar cheese (or hot pepper cheese for a kick)

5 eggs

¾ cup milk

⅛ teaspoon white pepper

¼ cup chopped red bell pepper

¼ cup chopped green bell pepper

¼ cup finely chopped onion

1 cup cubed cooked Burgers' Country Ham

Melt butter in an 8x8-inch glass baking dish. Add croutons; toss to coat. Sprinkle cheese over croutons. In a large bowl, beat eggs, milk and pepper; stir in bell peppers and onion. Pour mixture over croutons and cheese; top with ham. Cover with plastic wrap; refrigerate overnight. Preheat oven to 375°. Bring casserole to room temperature. Bake 40 to 45 minutes, until eggs are set. Rest 5 minutes before serving. Can also be frozen (microwave to warm later). Serves 4 to 5 people.

Family Favorite

Fun Fact:

There are two types of country hams offered at Burgers' Smokehouse. The Southern Smokehouse Country Ham .which is aged four to six months and then gently smoked. results in a mild, yet authentic country ham flavor. The Attic Aged Ham is aged for a minimum of seven months, creating a robust flavor sought by country ham connoisseurs.

JJ's at the Copper Pot

630 North Main Street
Gravois Mills, MO 65037
573-374-8077
jjsatthecopperpot.com
Find us on Facebook

JJ's offers lobster and prime rib and specializes in an American menu with international flair under the helm of the area's best chef, Joseph Cope. Certified Angus Beef is provided to ensure top quality, and the menu includes fresh salmon, local trout and weekly fish and seafood options. Exotic game is also prepared for the weekly, featured menu. The Copper Pot boasts a list of a 140+ unique wines, craft cocktails and a vast supply of popular and obscure liquors. You'll enjoy live entertainment Thursday through Saturday in the lounge and a comfortable, upscale atmosphere all around. Located around the best recreational lake in the country, JJ's is truly a dining destination.

Winter Hours:
Thursday–Saturday: 5:00 pm to 8:30 pm
Summer Hours:
Tuesday–Saturday: 5:00 pm to 9:00 pm

Tiramisu

Tiramisu is an excellent dessert for entertaining as it may be prepared in advance. It may be simply plated for a delicious treat or adorned with spun sugar for an elegant finish to an evening.

16 ounces mascarpone cheese

1¼ cups sugar

3 eggs, separated

3 packages ladyfingers

2½ cups strong cold coffee

1½ ounces Kahlua

1½ ounces brandy

1 tablespoon cocoa powder

Gently mix cheese, sugar and egg yolks together until smooth. Whisk egg whites until firm; fold into cheese mixture. Soak ladyfingers in coffee, Kahlua and brandy (quickly so the biscuit does not crumble). In a walled serving dish, tureen or baking dish, place layer ladyfingers. Top with thin layer of sweetened cheese mixture. Place another layer of soaked ladyfingers down, finishing with the rest of the mascarpone. Refrigerate at least 2 hours. Top with cocoa powder. Garnish with chocolate curls or warm chocolate sauce, if desired.

Restaurant Recipe

O'Donoghue's Steaks and Seafood

900 East High Street
Jefferson City, MO 65101
573-635-1332
www.odonoghuesrestaurant.com

O'Donoghue's Steaks and Seafood, located in Jefferson City's historic 1895 Kaullen Mercantile Company building, specializes in steaks and seafood. O'Donoghue's lends itself to a historic atmosphere with original red oak floors, pocket doors, and original fluted iron columns. They are now part of the National Register of Historic Places. This is one of the favorite places people gather over good food and drinks to share ideas and ideologies, milestones and memories, and of course politics, the lifeblood of Jefferson City. You only have to experience O'Donoghue's once to realize it is truly a one-of-a-kind place to eat, meet people, and relax.

Monday–Friday: 11:00 am to 9:00 pm
Saturdays: 4:00 pm to 10:00 pm

Lemon Drop Martini

1 ounce Absolut Citron

1 ounce Triple Sec

1 ounce limoncello

1 squeeze of fresh lemon

3 ounces sweet and sour

Mix with ice in shaker; shake vigorously. Pour into a frozen martini glass with a sugar rim. Garnish with a fresh lemon wedge.

Restaurant Recipe

Key Lime Martini

1½ ounces Absolut vanilla vodka

1 ounce Triple Sec

Dash Rose's Lime

Heaping tablespoon powdered sugar

4 ounces sweet and sour

Mix with ice in shaker; shake vigorously. Pour into a frozen martini glass with a powdered sugar rim. Garnish with a fresh lime wedge.

Restaurant Recipe

Simple Crème Brûlée

16 egg yolks, beaten

1¼ cups sugar, plus more for garnish

Mix sugar and egg yolks

1 quart heavy cream

Pinch kosher salt

1 ounce pure vanilla extract

Beat yolks and sugar together; set aside. Bring cream to a scald in a saucepan. Temper in the egg mixture; add salt. Mix in vanilla. Pour mixture in 8 ramekins resting in a shallow water bath in oven. Cover with sheet pan. Bake at 350° for 1 hour and 15 minutes; uncover and bake for 6 to 8 minutes. Pour off water bath; refrigerate for at least 2 hours. Spread sugar around top; torch until dark and crispy.

Restaurant Recipe

NOT THE PLACE YOU WANT TO BE

Missouri State Penitentiary Tours, Jefferson City

Missouri State Penitentiary has a long and disturbing history. Its long history began when it first opened in 1836. At that time, the Battle of the Alamo was going on in Texas, and Andrew Jackson was in his second term as president. When Alcatraz began taking in inmates, Missouri State Penitentiary had already been housing convicts for 100 years.

Prison riots, fires, notorious prisoners, murders on the grounds, death row inmates housed in below ground cells...it is no wonder that in 1967, the "Missouri State Pen" was named the "bloodiest 47 acres in America" by *Time* magazine.

Now that you know the history, let's talk about your present-day visit to the penitentiary. No, it's not your mom's worst nightmare...it's a unique look at what was once one of the oldest continually operated penitentiaries. You will see some of the older sections of the State Pen with tour guides who used to work within the walls of the penitentiary as corrections officers and guards. Your visit could even feature a past inmate recounting what it was like to serve time there.

Tours include the dungeon cells—pitch black rooms below ground—and the gas chamber, which was used up until 1989 to execute prisoners. Prison tours might allow you to visit cells of famous inmates. Sonny Liston learned to box within the walls and eventually became a heavyweight champion. James Earl Ray was admitted to the penitentiary March 17, 1960. On April 23, 1967, prisoner #00416J escaped in a bread box that was supposed to contain loaves of bread being transported to Renz prison. During the trip, Ray escaped and was later convicted for the assassination of Martin Luther King, Jr. in 1968.

If all that's not scary enough, plan a Twilight Ghost Tour for a nighttime visit or a Ghost Hunting Tour for an overnight stay on the grounds.

Missouri State Penitentiary Tours
115 Lafayette Street
Jefferson City, MO 65101
Operated by Jefferson City Convention & Visitors Bureau
866-998-6998
www.missouripentours.com

FUN FACTS:

- Opened in 1836.

- Housed 5,200 inmates at its peak.

- Once the largest prison in the United States.

- Served Missouri for 168 years; from 1836–2004.

- Bonnie Heady was the only woman to be executed in the gas chamber in a double execution, alongside Carl Hall, for the Greenlease killing.

- The facility opened for business in March 1836, the same month as the fall of the Alamo in Texas.

- Charles Arthur "Pretty Boy" Floyd entered M.S.P. on December 18, 1925, for a robbery.

- In 1974, Lillian Bonds became the first female Correctional Officer to work in a male correctional facility.

- Warden Donald "D.W." Wyrick was the youngest, longest tenured, and last "official" warden of the Missouri State Penitentiary.

- From 1938 to 1965, thirty nine prisoners were executed in the penitentiary's gas chamber.

Panheads BBQ and Tavern

5701 Old US Highway 40
Kingdom City, MO 65262
573-642-4800
www.facebook.com/PanheadsBbqTavern

Panheads BBQ and Tavern is committed to offering excellent homemade cooking with the freshest ingredients available in the region. The breads are made by a local bakery, making the sandwiches even better, and the ice cream is made by a local apiary that uses honey instead of sugar. Smoking the pork ribs, beef brisket, and pulled pork over 16 hours using hickory wood and very little rub lets the customer taste the smoky and natural juices of the meats, and makes them tender and juicy. Panheads is committed to offering fresh, prime-quality, homemade-from-scratch foods. Come and check them out, and don't forget to try the freshly made barbecue sauces, too.

Wednesday–Saturday: 11:00 am to 9:30 pm
Sunday: Noon to 8:00 pm

Easy Baked Beans

1 small onion, chopped
2 tablespoons cider vinegar
1 (16-ounce) can baked beans
1 (15-ounce) can pork and beans
⅓ cup barbecue sauce
1 cup chopped burnt ends

In a 2-quart saucepan over medium heat, cook onion and vinegar 3 to 5 minutes until onion is tender. Stir in remaining ingredients; heat to boiling. Reduce heat to medium low; cook uncovered 5 minutes, stirring occasionally.

Restaurant Recipe

Easy Coleslaw

½ cup mayonnaise
2 tablespoons white sugar
1½ tablespoons lemon juice
1 tablespoon vinegar
½ teaspoon black pepper
¼ tablespoon salt
¼ tablespoon horseradish paste
1 (16-ounce) bag slaw mix

Whisk together all ingredients, except slaw mix, until smooth and creamy. Pour over slaw mix, distributing evenly. Cool in refrigerator for an hour or until ready to serve.

Restaurant Recipe

Stewart's Restaurant

2 LOCATIONS:
1151 Bagnell Dam Boulevard
Lake Ozark, MO 65049
573-365-2400

98 East Highway 54
Camdenton, MO 65020
573-873-2900

Stewart's Restaurant is a classic example of local food at its best, just friendly service and great food. They are known for the biggest buns at the lake; I'm talking about cinnamon buns as big as your head. Enjoy the omelets, breakfast sandwiches, burgers, and tenderloin sandwiches. You won't walk away hungry. Stewart's is one of the top fourteen must-dos at the lake, was just voted one of the top 21 restaurants to visit while in Missouri, and was voted Best Breakfast Place at the Lake. Get there early if you don't want to wait, but, like all good things, they are worth the wait.

7 days a week: 6:00 am to 2:00 pm

Traditionally

Stewart's
RESTAURANT

Since 1953

Turtle Pumpkin Pie

¼ cup plus 2 tablespoons
caramel topping, divided

1 graham cracker pie crust

½ cup plus 2 tablespoons
chopped pecans, divided

2 (3.4-ounce) packages vanilla pudding

1 cup cold milk

1 cup canned pumpkin

1 teaspoon cinnamon

½ teaspoon nutmeg

1 (8-ounce) carton Cool Whip, divided

Pour ¼ cup caramel topping onto
crust; sprinkle with ½ cup nuts. Whisk
together pudding mix, milk, pumpkin,
cinnamon and nutmeg. Fold in 1½ cups
Cool Whip. Pour into pie crust. Chill 1
hour. Top with remaining Cool Whip,
caramel topping and pecans.

Restaurant Recipe

Loaded Cherry Pie

1 (21-ounce) can cherry pie filling

1 (20-ounce) can crushed
pineapple with juice

¾ cup sugar

3 tablespoons cornstarch

1 (3-ounce) box cherry gelatin (Jell-O)

4 bananas, sliced

1 cup chopped pecans

2 pie crusts, baked

1 (16-ounce) carton Cool Whip

In a saucepan, combine pie filling,
pineapple, sugar and cornstarch. Cook
until thick; remove from heat. Add
gelatin; stir to dissolve. Cool. Add
bananas and pecans. Pour into cooled
pie shells; top with Cool Whip.

Restaurant Recipe

Charley's Buffet

23785 Highway B
Lincoln, MO 65338
660-668-3806
www.facebook.com/Charleys-Buffet

Located in the middle of nowhere, down by Lake of the Ozarks, Charley's is an "all homemade" buffet. They serve home-style foods, such as pan-fried chicken, smothered steak, ham, roast beef, fried tators, fried noodles, sauerkraut, baked beans, and lots of other goodies, including a dessert bar with an average of 50 different pies, cookies, cakes, bars, and cream cheese varieties to choose from. Family owned since 1998, Charley's was started on the fundamentals of God, family, and good food. Recipes passed down for generations reflect these concepts and are the foundation for Charley's Buffet. Some things should never change, good food being one of them.

Friday & Saturday: 4:30 pm to 8:30 pm except Thanksgiving Day 11:00 am to 3:00 pm
Open March through Thanksgiving

Baked Steak

½ cup all-purpose flour

Salt and pepper to taste

1 tenderized round steak,
trimmed and cut into portions

Oil for frying

2 (10.75-ounce) cans cream
of mushroom soup

2 cans water

1 envelope beefy onion soup mix

1 tablespoon Kitchen Bouquet

Mix together flour, salt and pepper for breading. Bread steak; fry in hot oil until golden brown. Place in glass baking dish. Mix remaining ingredients together; pour over meat. Cover; bake at 275° for several hours or on 350° for 1 hour, or until meat can be cut with a fork and sauce has slightly thickened.

Restaurant Recipe

Dinner Rolls (aka Buns)

2 (.25-ounce) envelopes
instant dry yeast

1 cup warm water

½ cup melted margarine

1½ cups warm milk, heated

1 cup sugar

2 teaspoons salt

7 cups bread flour

Dissolve yeast in water; set aside 10 minutes. Melt margarine and milk in a small saucepan over medium heat; set aside to cool while yeast is resting. When yeast is ready, add milk mixture. Add sugar, salt and flour—do not overwork dough. Let rise until doubled; punch down. Let rise again. Roll out, cut into triangles and roll into crescents or shape according to preference. Let formed rolls rise. Bake at 400° for 10 minutes.

Note: For cinnamon buns, sprinkle with milk, cinnamon and sugar after rolling out (but before cutting and forming).

Restaurant Recipe

SURE...WHEN PIGS FLY

Where Pigs Fly Farm, Linn

Linn is home to Cindy Brenneke and her Where Pigs Fly Farm, which features a huge menagerie of free-roaming animals.

Of course, her farm doesn't feature true airborne pigs. It is a rural petting zoo where people of all ages can mingle with farm animals, enjoy being outside, and experience life on the farm. You will encounter horses, goats, cats, dogs, donkeys, llamas, ducks, cows, and even some pigs. Despite the name, Cindy says she's really not "that into pigs." Of course, sometimes your destiny develops wings of its own. Which is why Cindy's farm is now also home to the only Pig Museum in America.

Through a series of crazy connections, Susi Hosna connected with Cindy to tell her about her deceased husband's pig collection. Ross Hosna was a policeman who had been collecting "pigs" (anything and everything with a pig on it) since the 1970s. His dying wish was to have his pig collection on public display, and his secondary goal was to break the record for the world's largest pig collection. So, the collection started with 14,500 pigs. But it didn't stop there.

Cindy has received pig collections from all over the United States: 3,000 pigs from Arizona, 4,000 from California, 7,000 from Louisiana, hundreds more from Indiana, Florida, Kansas, and even Italy. Her goal is to surpass a museum in Germany that has 40,000 pigs. Every visitor is encouraged to bring a pig to add to the collection, so watch out Germany, Cindy's collections will bypass you when pigs fly...wait, I mean Where Pigs Fly.

Where Pigs Fly Farm
314-241-3488
www.wherepigsflyfarm.com

Because kids don't remember their best day watching TV

Where Pigs Fly Farm
Pigs Aloft Museum

Farm & Museum Tours
Petting Zoo
Private Parties
Bed & Breakfast

314-241-3488

www.WherePigsFlyFarm.com

FUN FACTS:

- You can spend the night on the farm—stay in one of the museum bedrooms, tent camp, or barn camp.

- The farm has more than 400 animals and birds for you to meet, including Grunt and Babe—two big hogs weighing more than 1,000 pounds each.

- Some of the more exotic animals include Amazon Parrots and Patagonian Cavies.

- Cindy also operates a camp—Where Pigs Fly Camp—for kids.

Willowes Bar & Grill

2010 State Road A
Linn Creek, MO 65052
573-346-6197
Find us on Facebook

Willowes Bar & Grill, located on State Road A in the very small town of Linn Creek, is owned by two sisters living out their dream of entrepreneurship, serving locals and tourists alike. Willowes has something for everyone—burgers, fries, pastas, steaks, and more. Nearly everything is made from scratch. Dine-in, carry-out, and catering are all available to make any occasion a memorable experience. They offer a full service bar served with a smile from the friendly and efficient staff in a place where everyone feels like family. Don't forget to ask about the fried potato salad.

Monday–Saturday: 10:00 am to 10:00 pm
Sunday: 10:00 am to 9:00 pm

Chicken Bacon Ranch Burger

5 pounds skinless boneless chicken

2 eggs, beaten

⅓ cup breadcrumbs

¾ cup shredded Cheddar Jack cheese

¾ cup cooked diced bacon

2 (1-ounce) packages dry ranch mix

Grind chicken in a meat grinder; add remaining ingredients. Mix well; form into burgers. Cook 5 to 6 minutes per side or until internal temperature reaches 165°.

Restaurant Recipe

Fried Chicken

1 chicken, cut into serving pieces

2 cups buttermilk

Seasoned flour

Oil for frying

In a baking dish, cook chicken at 350° for 1 hour. Cool enough to handle; dip in buttermilk and seasoned flour. Cook in 350° vegetable oil 5 to 6 minutes.

Restaurant Recipe

Spiced Bread Pudding

8 eggs

3 cups milk

1½ cups heavy cream

2 cups sugar

1 teaspoon vanilla

1 loaf cinnamon raisin bread, cubed

Wisk together eggs, milk, heavy cream, sugar and vanilla; add bread to custard mixture. Pour into a 9x13-inch pan; bake at 350° for 1 hour.

Sauce:

1 stick butter, melted

½ cup brown sugar

1 teaspoon cinnamon

¼ cup heavy cream

In a saucepan, stir together butter, brown sugar, cinnamon and heavy cream; simmer until sauce reduces and thickens. Top bread pudding with sauce.

Restaurant Recipe

The Cook Shack BBQ & More

8827 Northeast State Highway ZZ
Osceola, MO 64776
417-646-5516
www.facebook.com/TheCookShack

The Cook Shack, located on Truman Lake, offers casual home-cooked dining at affordable prices. Just look around "The Shack" to see why "unique" is their middle name. You'll enter a by-gone era when things were simpler, more casual, and definitely more relaxed. The building, which started as a carport, now includes a cargo shipping container that serves as the kitchen, and the attached garden shed is used to house the dry storage and a restroom. Take a whiff. Smell that smoke? The menu is simple, but don't forget the Hillbilly melt, a thick slice of smoked bologna grilled and served on garlic toast with cheese, onions, and jalapeños. Enjoy daily specials while enjoying a fun, casual, family-friendly atmosphere serving smokin' barbecue and more.

Seasonal Hours:
May–August:
Thursday–Saturday: 11:00 am to 8:00 pm
Sundays: 11:00 am to 5:00 pm

September–April:
Friday & Saturday 11:00 am to 8:00 pm
Sundays: 11:00 am to 5:00 pm

Hillbilly Melt & Kickin' Cole Slaw

Killer Chocolate Cake

2 cups all-purpose flour

½ teaspoon salt

1 teaspoon baking powder

2 teaspoons baking soda

¾ cup unsweetened cocoa

2 cups sugar

1 cup vegetable oil

1 cup hot coffee

1 cup milk

2 eggs

1 teaspoon vanilla extract

Sift dry ingredients into mixing bowl; add oil, coffee and milk. Mix at medium speed 2 minutes. Add eggs and vanilla; beat 2 minutes more (batter will be thin). Pour into 2 greased and floured 9-inch cake pans. Bake at 350° for 25 to 30 minutes or until toothpick inserted in center comes out clean. Cool; frost with Killer Chocolate Frosting.

Killer Chocolate Frosting:

1 egg plus 1 egg yolk

1½ cups sugar

3 tablespoons melted butter

4½ tablespoons milk

3 tablespoons vegetable oil

½ cup plus 1 tablespoon unsweetened cocoa, sifted

Mix all ingredients; boil 2 to 3 minutes over low heat while stirring constantly. Cool and pour over cake.

Restaurant Recipe

Kickin' Coleslaw

1 head green cabbage, coarse shred

1 cup diced bell pepper

1 cup diced onion

2 cups julienned carrots

Dressing:

4 teaspoons celery seed

4 teaspoons salt

2 teaspoons black pepper

½ cup apple cider vinegar

½ cup sugar

3 cups mayonnaise

Combine, cabbage, bell pepper, onion and carrots; set aside. In another bowl, combine Dressing ingredients; keep separate until ready to serve.

Restaurant Recipe

Café Korea

839 VFW Memorial Drive, Suite 9
St. Robert, MO 65584
573-336-3232
Cafékorea.net
Find us on Facebook

Café Korea is a family restaurant serving authentic Korean cuisine, offering dine-in and carry-out service. Folks are looking for good food at a decent price—that is what Café Korea strives to offer. Quality is what keeps people coming back, whether quality of product or quality of service—they are in the business of both. Café Korea found the sweet spot in quality, and that is what has contributed to their continued success. As a result, anyone can share in and enjoy the delightful taste of genuine Korean food, prepared to order directly from the café kitchen.

Monday–Friday: 10:00 am to 8:00 pm

Bulgogi

¼ pear

4 cloves garlic

½ onion, halved, sliced into medium moon-shaped slivers and divided

1 kiwi fruit

¼ cup cola

2 pounds rib-eye steak or prime beef, thinly sliced

6 tablespoons soy sauce

3 tablespoons sugar

2 tablespoons cooking wine

½ teaspoon black pepper

1 teaspoon sesame oil

2 teaspoons olive oil, divided

1¼ carrot, thinly sliced

¼ cup chopped scallions,

1 teaspoon sesame seeds

In a food processor, combine pear, garlic, half the onion, kiwi and cola; process until well mixed. In a large bowl, add processed mixture and meat; mix well. Add soy sauce, sugar, wine, pepper, sesame oil and 1 teaspoon olive oil. Cover; refrigerate overnight. In a skillet over medium heat, add 1 teaspoon oil, meat mixture, carrot, remaining onion, and scallions. Cook meat 80% done; add sesame seeds and continue cooking until done.

Restaurant Recipe

Easy Cucumber Kimchi

1 pound cucumbers, halved lengthwise and sliced crosswise ¼-inch thick

1 teaspoon salt

½ small onion, thinly sliced

2 scallions, chopped

2 teaspoons gochugaru (Korean red pepper powder)

4 garlic cloves, minced

2 teaspoons sugar

2 tablespoons Heinz vinegar

1 teaspoon sesame seeds

1n a large bowl, mix and toss sliced cucumbers with all ingredients. Serve immediately, or chill and serve.

Restaurant Recipe

Sweetwater Bar-B-Que

14076 Highway Z
St. Robert, MO 65584
573-336-8830
www.sweetwater-bar-b-que.com
Find us on Facebook

Sweetwater Bar-B-Que is a small unique family owned and operated smokehouse located in the foothills of the Ozarks on Old Route 66. Although the building looks like it has been there for years, it was constructed in 1998, by the six Batchler children, stone by stone. This venture was taking a dream and making it a reality. The exterior was constructed with Missouri limestone and the interior floors and flagstones from the rivers of Arkansas. Don't get caught trying to pick up the silver dollars in the floor; they were given for good luck from their mom. Sweetwater provides finger-lickin' barbeque at a fair price.

Open daily: 11:00 am to 8:00 pm
Winter months closed on Mondays

Judy's Everything Carrot Cake

2 cups all-purpose flour

2 cups sugar

2 teaspoons cinnamon

2 teaspoons baking soda

¾ cup oil

¾ cup buttermilk

4 eggs, beaten

3 cups shredded carrots

1 (12-ounce) can crushed pineapple, drained

1 cup chopped walnuts

1 cup shredded coconut

¾ cup golden raisins

Preheat oven to 350°. Grease a 9x13-inch casserole dish, line with parchment and dust with flour; remove excess flour. In a large bowl, combine flour, sugar, cinnamon and baking soda; mix well. Add oil, buttermilk and eggs; mix well. Add carrots, pineapple, nuts, coconut and raisins; mix well. Pour into prepared dish; bake 40 to 50 minutes. Remove from heat; cool 15 minutes. Turn cake out; cool completely.

Cream Cheese Frosting:

1 stick butter, softened

1 (8-ounce) package cream cheese, softened

1 (16-ounce) package powdered sugar

½ teaspoon vanilla

Whip butter and cream cheese until fluffy. Add powdered sugar and vanilla; whip until fluffy. Spread over cake.

Restaurant Recipe

Sweetwater Hillbilly Beans

½ cup chopped bacon

½ cup diced onion, white or yellow

½ cup water

½ cup packed brown sugar

1 (115-ounce) can baked beans

In a skillet, brown bacon until resembles bacon bits; add onion, cooking until translucent. Add water and sugar; cook until sugar is dissolved. Pour beans into a large pot; add bacon-onion mixture. Cook until heated through.

Restaurant Recipe

The Mason Jar Café

217 South Ohio Avenue
Sedalia, MO 65301
660-829-5054
Find us on Facebook

Ever wanted to find a Goddess in the kitchen? The Mason Jar Café is the place to go. Ms. Penny has been called that by many people that come in for the delicious foods being served from her kitchen. From biscuits and gravy in the morning and strawberry scones that melt in your mouth, to the many plate lunch specials that are just like Mama cooked when you were a kid. You will be impressed with the tasteful melding of old and new in the décor. The original tin ceiling and old fashioned soda counter; tells a story of their own.

Tuesday–Friday: 7:00 am to 2:00 pm
Saturday: 9:00 am to 2:00 pm

Harvest Caramel Apple Dump Cake

2 (20-ounce) cans apple pie filling
2 teaspoons ground cinnamon
1 teaspoon ground nutmeg
1½ cups caramel bits
1 box yellow cake mix
¾ cup butter, softened

Preheat oven to 350°. In a medium bowl, combine pie filling, cinnamon and nutmeg. Pour into a greased 9x13-inch pan; spread with spatula. Sprinkle with caramel bits; evenly top with dry cake mix. Top cake with thin slices of butter evenly spaced. (You can add more cinnamon on top if you like.) Bake 45 minutes or until top is lightly browned and edges are bubbling. Serve with a scoop of ice cream or warm caramel sauce.

Restaurant Recipe

Sun Dried Tomato Basil Hummus

Fresh basil to taste
Garlic powder to taste
3 to 4 tablespoons lemon juice
2 tablespoons tahini
½ teaspoon salt
3 cups sun dried tomatoes
2 tablespoons oil from sun dried tomatoes
1 (15-ounce) can garbanzo beans

Combine ingredients into a large food processor; pulse 1 minute. Scrape sides; pulse an additional 3 minutes. If not smooth enough, drizzle in olive oil or more lemon juice. Serve with bread, crackers or even vegetables. Enjoy.

Restaurant Recipe

Vichy Wye Restaurant

13990 Highway 63 South
Vichy, MO 65580
573-299-4720
Find us on Facebook

If you are looking for a genuine gem in the rough, go no further than Vichy Wye Restaurant in Vichy. This is truly a perfect family dining experience serving the best patty melt—it gets better each time you eat it—burgers, plate lunches, catfish, steaks, and pork tenderloins, and the weekend buffet is always the best anywhere. For more than 20 years, Ms. Viki and the gang have served good food with a pleasant dining experience. Don't forget the quarter coffees and delectable pies. Everything is always home-cooked to perfection. This is a fine example of the full-meal café that is so hard to find in today's world.

7 days a week: 11:00 am to 8:00 pm

Chicken and Dumplings

1 whole fresh chicken
1½ cups chicken base
Salt and pepper to taste
Pinch baking powder
6 cups all-purpose flour, divided

Clean chicken, removing the wing tips, fat, neck and back bone. In a stockpot, place chicken, cover with water and add base; bring to a boil. Cook until chicken is fork-tender; taste for salt and chicken taste. Add pepper and more salt if needed. Remove chicken from broth; set aside. Take out 3 cups broth; cool to "baby bottle temp." In a large bowl, add cooled broth, baking powder and 3 cups flour, 1 cup at a time, stirring until flour is absorbed. Set aside 10 minutes. On a flat surface, spread the other 3 cups flour, pour out ⅓ flour mixture. Flour your rolling pin; start rolling. Constantly flip more flour over rolled portion and pin to keep from sticking. Roll as thin as you can, but still be able to pick the mixture off the flat surface. Cut strips with a pizza cutter into dumpling size. Repeat until all mixture is rolled and cut. Gently drop dumplings into gently rolling broth, one at a time making sure there is broth between dumplings. After last dumpling is dropped, cook another 10 minutes; turn off heat. Return chicken to pot and serve.

Family Favorite

Homemade Coconut Cream Pie

3½ cups milk

½ stick margarine

¾ cup all-purpose flour

¾ cup sugar

Pinch salt

4 eggs, separated

1 teaspoon vanilla

¾ cup flaked coconut

1 pre-baked pie crust, cooled

Preheat oven to 400°. In a medium saucepan over medium heat, combine milk, margarine, flour, sugar, salt, egg yolks (reserve whites for Meringue) and vanilla; stir with a whisk until pudding starts to thicken. Add ¾ cup coconut; mixing well. Pour into pie crust; set aside while making Meringue.

Meringue:

4 egg whites

Pinch salt

¼ teaspoon cream of tartar

½ cup sugar

¼ cup flaked coconut

In a mixing bowl, using an electric mixer on medium speed, whip egg whites, salt and cream of tartar until frothy. Slowly add sugar. After all sugar is added, turn mixer on high; beat until stiff peaks form. Top pie, making sure to seal edges. Garnish with coconut. Cook in oven for 10 minutes or until coconut is browned. Refrigerate at least 2 hours before serving.

Restaurant Recipe

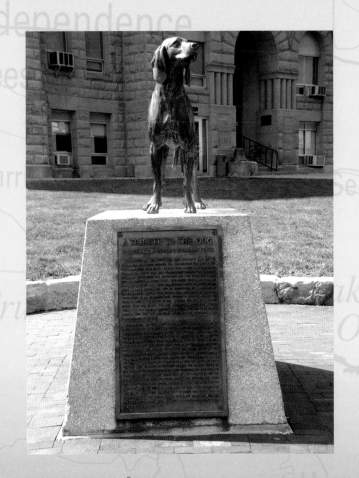

MAN'S BEST FRIEND
Statue of Old Drum, Warrensburg

Chances are, if you haven't used it yourself, you have definitely heard the expression "man's best friend" as referred to a dog. But do you know the inspiration for the expression? It all starts with a beloved dog, a heinous shooting, and four trials featuring prominent legal counsel. The subject of this trial—Old Drum—is immortalized in a statue on the lawn of the Johnson County Courthouse in Warrensburg.

Old Drum was a hound dog owned by Charles Burden. One night in 1869, Old Drum wandered onto neighboring property and was shot dead by Samuel "Dick" Ferguson, nephew and ward of Leonidas Hornsby. Hornsby, who happened to be Burden's brother-in-law, thought the dog had been killing his sheep. Burden sued Hornsby, sparking a highly charged and emotional legal battle culminating in a Supreme Court decision in favor of Burden.

The trial became one of the strangest in the history of Missouri with each man determined to win the case. The original jury was hung. The second trial resulted in a guilty verdict, and Burden was awarded $25 plus court costs. Hornsby appealed. New lawyers were hired. And, on April 1, 1870, Hornsby was found not guilty and awarded court costs. But the saga was not over.

On September 21, 1870, in Warrensburg, the case of Old Drum went to trial for the fourth time. It was in the courtroom that Burden's lawyer, future senator George Graham Vest, delivered his famous "eulogy to the dog." The speech included the line, "The one absolutely unselfish friend that a man can have in this selfish world, the one that never deserts him, the one that never proves ungrateful or treacherous, is his dog."

In the end, Burden was awarded $50—the maximum amount of damages allowed by the law at the time. Old Drum will remain in the hearts of dog lovers everywhere. Thanks to coordinated efforts from the Warrensburg Chamber of Commerce and dog lovers from around the country, Old Drum was immortalized in a bronze statue, which was completed on September 23, 1958. So, the next time you use the term, "man's best friend," remember Old Drum.

Johnson County Courthouse
102 South Holden Street
Warrensburg, MO 64093
(at the corner of Hout Street and North Holden Street;
Southeast corner of courthouse square)

Heroes
Restaurant & Pub

107 West Pine Street
Warrensburg, MO 64093
660-747-3162
www.heroeswarrensburg.com
Find us on Facebook

In 2016, Heroes Restaurant celebrated 35 years in Downtown Warrensburg. Fresh food is the mantra and the secret to their success. Homemade onion rings and hand-pattied burgers top the list. The four buildings that house Heroes Restaurant are vintage 1880 and full of lots of interesting old stuff. The Scullys and Wards, the original owners, are still part of the daily operations. That's why Heroes is a Pine Street legend since 1981.

Monday–Thursday:
11:00 am to 10:00 pm
Friday & Saturday: 11:00 am to 11:00 pm
Sunday: 10:00 am to 9:00 pm
Pub Hours 7 days a week:
11:00 am to 1:00 am

Heroes Homemade BBQ Meatballs

1¼ pounds ground ham
1 pound pork sausage
½ pound ground beef
1½ cups graham cracker crumbs
2 eggs, beaten
1 cup milk
1 cup ketchup
1 cup brown sugar
2 tablespoons white vinegar
1 tablespoon dried mustard

Combine ham, sausage, beef, crumbs, eggs and milk by hand until thoroughly mixed; shape into 1-inch balls. Mix ketchup, sugar, vinegar and mustard; pour over meatballs. Bake at 350° for 1 hour.

Restaurant Recipe

Heroes Cheesecake

Crust:

1½ cups graham cracker crumbs

¼ cup melted margarine

¼ cup sugar

Mix together; press into 8- or 9-inch springform pan. Make Batter.

Batter:

5 (8-ounce) packages cream cheese, softened

1 cup sugar

4 eggs

1 teaspoon vanilla

Mix cream cheese and sugar until smooth, scraping sides often. Add eggs, 1 at a time, mixing well after each. Add vanilla; mix 5 to 8 more minutes. Pour mixture over Crust; bake at 350° for 30 to 40 minutes or until toothpick comes out clean. Cool before topping.

Topping:

2 cups sour cream

¼ cup sugar

1 teaspoon vanilla

Mix ingredients; pour over baked and cooled cake. Bake at 275° for 5 minutes.

Restaurant Recipe

Barbie's Crabbie Dip

This is my sister Barb's dip. She is not crabby too often.

3 (8-ounce) packages cream cheese, softened

4 ounces crabmeat (can use imitation)

½ cup chopped green onions

¾ cup sour cream

½ teaspoon granulated garlic

1 teaspoon Worcestershire sauce

¾ cup grated Parmesan cheese

1 cup half-and-half

Mix all ingredients; pour into a greased 9x13-inch pan. Bake at 350° until top browns. Makes ½ gallon. Serve with fried wontons for dipping.

Family Recipe

Southwestern REGION

157

Autumn's Café and Grille

207 Northwest 12th Avenue
Ava, MO 65608
417-683-1280
www.autumnscafégrille.com

It all started with a dream and a prayer. Autumn's Café & Grille, created in 2012, has quickly become the favorite family gathering spot for the community of Ava. Autumn's provides traditional, American-style food, offering breakfast, lunch, and dinner seven days a week in a relaxed atmosphere. They are known for their breakfast, burgers, steaks, fresh-ground coffee, desserts, soups, salad bar, and rolls. Try the country-fried steak, the Foxtrotter skillet, or the Hillbilly. Come see the talk of the locals and enjoy a home-cooked meal next time you're in town.

Tuesday–Wednesday: 7:00 am to 3:00 pm
Thursday–Monday: 7:00 am to 8:00 pm

White Beans

2 pounds white beans
4 quarts water
5 to 6 sprigs fresh oregano
1 white onion
½ cup minced garlic
½ cup bacon grease
Salt to taste

Soak beans overnight in water; drain. Place beans in a stockpot; add 4 quarts water, oregano, onion, garlic and bacon grease. Bring to a boil; simmer uncovered until desired tenderness, adding more water as needed. Salt to taste.

Family Favorite

Asparagus with Orange and Cashew Cream Sauce

1½ pounds fresh asparagus
4 tablespoons butter
4 tablespoons flour
2 cups milk
1 fresh orange, sectioned
½ cup chopped cashews

Cook asparagus in salted water until tender; drain. In a saucepan, melt butter; add flour, stirring until blended. Gradually add milk, stirring constantly; cook until thick and smooth. Add orange sections and cashews.

Family Favorite

Skillet Potatoes

5 potatoes, peeled
¼ cup vegetable oil
2 onions, julienned and sautéed
2 leeks, chopped and sautéed
1½ cups chopped, cooked bacon
5 eggs, whipped
4 tablespoons chopped fresh sage
Salt and pepper to taste

Boil whole potatoes to three quarters done; shred. Heat oil in a cast iron skillet. Combine all ingredients in a bowl; mix well. Pour into skillet. Cook until golden brown; flip. Cook other side until golden brown.

Family Favorite

True Brew LLC

130 East Washington Avenue
Ava, MO 65608
417-683-4500
www.facebook.com/TrueBrewLLC/

True Brew LLC is a bistro-café offering a variety of specialty coffee drinks and hand-crafted foods. Their goal is to offer an excellent array of quality beverages, as well as more health-conscience food options to the community. From hand-mixed Italian sodas to the artisan turkey sandwich, everything is prepared fresh to order. Whether you're passing through Ava on your way to the Laura Ingalls Wilder home, or headed down to Bull Shoals Lake, here's a menu worth stopping for.

Monday–Friday: 7:00 am to 6:00 pm
Saturday: 8:00 am to 2:00 pm

Berry Patch Smoothie

2 ounces plain Greek yogurt
1 tablespoon raw honey
2 ounces frozen banana slices
2 ounces frozen whole strawberries
2 ounces frozen blueberries
8 ounces almond milk
2 ounces organic granola (optional)

In a blender, add Greek yogurt and honey. Add bananas, strawberries and blueberries; pour milk over the top. Blend until smooth. Enjoy. Make it into a delicious and filling breakfast option by putting your smoothie into a larger sized glass and adding granola to the top; mix it in with a spoon. Makes 1 (16-ounce) smoothie.

Restaurant Recipe

Snickerdoodles

2⅔ cups all-purpose flour

1 teaspoon cream of tartar

1 teaspoon baking soda

¼ teaspoon salt

½ cup butter-flavored
Crisco shortening

½ cup unsalted butter

1½ cups plus 1 tablespoon
sugar, divided

1 teaspoon pure vanilla extract

2 large eggs

1 tablespoon cinnamon

Preheat oven to 400°. Mix together, flour, cream of tartar, baking soda and salt; set aside. With an electric mixer, cream shortening, butter and 1½ cups sugar on medium speed until fluffy; add vanilla. Add eggs, one at a time. Add dry ingredients in 3 increments. Mix 1 tablespoon sugar and cinnamon in a bowl. Roll dough into 1- to 1½-inch balls; coat with sugar mixture. Place balls 2 inches apart on baking sheet; gently press down center of ball with a wide spoon. Bake 8 to 10 minutes.

**Family Favorite and
Restaurant Recipe**

At DANNA'S our ribs are BIG, BOLD & VERY MEATY.

Danna's Bar B Que and Burger Shop

3 LOCATIONS

963 State Highway 165
Branson, MO 65616
417-337-5527
Monday–Saturday: 10:30 am to 9:00 pm

15 Hope Way
Branson West, MO 65737
417-272-1945
Monday–Saturday: 11:00 am to 9:00 pm

7930 East Highway 76
Kirbyville, MO 65679
417-334-9541
Monday–Saturday: 11:00 am to 9:00 pm
Sunday: 11:00 am to 3:00 pm

Danna's, family owned and run, is well known for being the place to go for old-fashioned, made-from-scratch barbecue. Beef and pork are smoked for 12 to 14 hours every night with locally sourced hickory wood. The ribs, chicken, and sausage are smoked for four hours twice a day, using their own barbecue rub and sauces, which are available for you to purchase. Burgers are made to order from fresh beef or turkey. Try the smoked pork plate piled high with tender pork and served with homemade coleslaw and signature Memphis rolls. Try the barbecue nachos or a Boss Man Salad along with a variety of sandwiches and burgers.

Bananas Foster

2 tablespoons unsalted butter

¼ cup dark brown sugar

¼ teaspoon ground allspice

½ teaspoon freshly ground nutmeg

1 tablespoon banana liqueur

**2 under ripe bananas, sliced
in half lengthwise**

¼ cup dark rum

½ teaspoon finely grated orange zest

Melt butter in a 10-inch heavy skillet over low heat. Add brown sugar, allspice and nutmeg; stir until sugar dissolves. Add liqueur; bring sauce to simmer. Add bananas; cook for 1 minute on each side, carefully spooning sauce over bananas while cooking. Remove bananas to serving dish. Bring sauce back to a simmer; carefully add rum. If the sauce is very hot, the alcohol will flame on its own. (If not, carefully ignite.) Continue cooking until flame dies, 1 to 2 minutes. If sauce is too thin, cook for another 1 to 2 minutes until syrupy in consistency. Add orange zest; stir to combine. Immediately spoon sauce over bananas. Serve with waffles, crêpes or ice cream.

Restaurant Recipe

Barbecue Rub

1 tablespoon kosher salt

1 tablespoon brown sugar

2 tablespoons chili powder

1 tablespoon black pepper

½ tablespoon cayenne pepper

1 tablespoon paprika

1 tablespoon seasoned salt

Thoroughly mix ingredients; rub on ribs or chicken before slow smoking over favorite wood.

Restaurant Recipe

Red Barn Café & Hen House Bakery

2845 State Highway 76
Branson, MO 65616
417-334-3032
Find us on Facebook

This Red Barn and Hen House Bakery is just like sitting at your grandmother's table. Enjoy whimsical charm and great service, along with southern foods you grew up eating. If you like the taste and smell of fried chicken, sizzling hot, fried catfish, and burgers made fresh, just the way you like them, Red Barn is the place for you. Before you leave, browse through our selection of baked goods. Take some home with you, and tell your husband you cooked them. Watch the surprise on his face. Full menu, buffet, private meeting room, and banquet areas, and catering, Red Barn has it all.

Monday–Saturday: 6:00 am to 9:00 pm
Sunday: 7:00 am to 3:00 pm

Carrot Cake

24 eggs

12 cups sugar

9 cups oil

12 cups all-purpose flour

4 tablespoons baking soda

1 tablespoon salt

2 tablespoons cinnamon

18 cups grated carrots

12 cups finely chopped nuts

In a large bowl, beat eggs and sugar until light and fluffy. Slowly add oil, beating well. In another bowl, mix flour, baking soda, salt and cinnamon. Blend dry ingredients into egg mixture. Add carrots and nuts. Bake in desired pans at 350° for 45 minutes, or until done.

Restaurant Recipe

Chocolate Silk Pie

½ pound walnuts, chopped

½ pound pecans, chopped

1 cup brown sugar

Pinch cinnamon

1¼ pounds butter, divided

1½ cups sugar

12 eggs

2½ pounds bittersweet chocolate, melted

½ cup heavy cream

Blend together walnuts, pecans, brown sugar, cinnamon and ½ pound butter; press into springform pan. Cream together ¾ pound butter and sugar; slowly add eggs, beating well after each egg. Mix in chocolate. Whip in heavy cream. Pour into baked pie crusts; refrigerate 24 hours; top with whipped topping.

Restaurant Recipe

Cream Cheese Frosting

6 (8-ounce) packages cream cheese, softened

3 cups butter, softened

6 (16-ounce) packages powdered sugar

4 tablespoons vanilla

Beat cream cheese and butter together until smooth. Add powdered sugar and vanilla. Beat until smooth.

Restaurant Recipe

Smith Creek Moonshine

1209 Branson Landing Boulevard
Branson, MO 65616
800-441-5053
www.smithcreekmoonshine.com

"Growing up in these here parts, my grandma always whipped up the most scrumptious, belly-warming, tongue-pleasing, delicious meals for all our family gatherings. Well, she didn't contribute a dang thing to these recipes. Here are some of MY recipes. Hope you're in the mood to make some of the best down-home grub you've ever eaten," as quoted by General Manager Johan Reggie Regnell. Enjoy.

Monday–Saturday: 10:00 am to 9:00 pm
Sunday: 10:00 am to 8:00 pm

Smith Creek BBQ Sauce

3½ cups ketchup

2 tablespoons soy sauce

2 tablespoons Worcestershire sauce

¾ cup brown sugar

½ cup water

¼ cup Smith Creek Straight Moonshine (optional or use water)

6 tablespoons apple cider vinegar

2 tablespoons browning sauce

2½ teaspoons dry mustard

1 teaspoon black pepper

½ teaspoon cumin

Mix all ingredients in a big pot. Bring to a boil; simmer 30 to 45 minutes, stirring occasionally.

Restaurant Recipe

Smith Creek Chili

1 white onion, finely chopped

2 cups finely chopped celery

1 tablespoon butter

1 pound ground beef

1 quart beef broth

4 ounces Smith Creek BBQ Sauce

½ cup ketchup

2½ tablespoons granulated garlic

2½ tablespoons chili powder

1 tablespoon paprika

1 tablespoon ground cumin

1 tablespoon black pepper

2 tomatoes, cubed

Sour cream

Shredded cheese

Chopped green onion

Sauté white onion and celery in butter until soft. Add ground beef; fry until brown. Add beef broth, Smith Creek BBQ Sauce and ketchup; stir until mixed. Mix in all spices. Add tomatoes; simmer for 45 minutes to 1 hour, stirring occasionally. Let chili sit for at least 5 minutes before serving. Garnish with sour cream, shredded cheese and chopped green onion. Enjoy.

Restaurant Recipe

A 200-ACRE COMMUNITY PARK OR WORKING FARM?

Rutledge-Wilson Farm Park, Springfield

Is it a park or farm? Yes, it is. Rutledge-Wilson Farm Park is a 207-acre park and farm, created by the Springfield-Greene County Park Board to provide educational and recreational resources, celebrating the rich agricultural heritage of the Ozarks in a fun and unique play space.

Opened in 2007, the centerpiece of the park is a 4,112 square-foot Big Red Barn, home to miniature horses, miniature donkeys, Nigerian Dwarf Goats, Boar Goats, and Dorper Sheep. The Barn also includes a veterinary office, tack room, hay storage, nine exterior corrals, a wash bay and a roomy classroom, which is busy with classes, visiting school groups, crafts, story hours and birthday parties.

The chicken coop, turkey enclosure, rabbit hutch and more animal pens are just outside the barn. Hogs and piglets live nearby in the Pig Palace, including their own barn and pen. Kids may visit Irene the Dairy Queen — a larger-than-life fiberglass Holstein milk cow. Irene may be filled with water to give visitors an opportunity to see what it is like to milk a cow.

Outside of the animals, attractions at the farm include a farm-themed playground, pedal tractors area, bonfire pits, and a picnic area. There are 70 acres of forage crops, rotated annually. A one-acre fishing pond is stocked with largemouth bass, bluegill and channel catfish for catch and release fishing. The Wilson's Creek Greenway, a paved recreation trail, crosses through the property.

The earliest recorded name of the owner of the property is Daniel N. Beal, who filed a federal land patent for the property. The farm changed hands multiple times before being passed down to namesake, John G. Wilson in 1944. In 1982, the Farm's ownership was passed onto namesake Troy Rutledge. The entire property was purchased by the City of Springfield in 2001. Rutledge-Wilson Farm Park opened to the public in 2007, and friends and families have been making "farm-tastic" memories there ever since.

Rutledge-Wilson Farm Community Park
3825 West Farm Road 146
Springfield, MO 65810
417-837-5949
www.parkboard.org/265/Rutledge-Wilson-Farm-Community-Park

Mary Lee's Café

710 West 20th Street
Joplin, MO 64804
417-623-9666
Find us on Facebook

Welcome to Mary Lee's Café in Joplin. This is one of the old school, true diners from days of long ago. This is just like sitting at your grandmother's table where you get your plate full, your belly full and your ears full from the gossip being passed around. Enter as a stranger, hear all the town talk, and enjoy the best omelets ever and a wide variety to boot—eggs, bacon, sausage, French toast, and biscuits with a side order of gravy. What more would you want? The portions are so large you can fill your tummy and have enough left over for an afternoon snack. Then there is lunch with fried chicken steak so tender it just about melts on the plate. Don't forget to try the Reuben. Everything here is made to order.

Monday–Saturday: 6:00 am to 1:30 pm
Sunday: 6:30 am to 1:30 pm

Goulash

2 pounds ground beef
½ onion, chopped
2 (10-ounce) cans Rotel tomatoes
1 (16-ounce) jar salsa
Pinch salt and pepper
1 (16-ounce) package elbow macaroni
1 (16-ounce) package
shredded Cheddar cheese

In a skillet, brown meat with onion. Add tomatoes, salsa, salt and pepper; simmer while you cook macaroni. Cook macaroni according to package directions till al dente; add to meat mixture. Pour into a 9x13-inch casserole; top with cheese. Bake at 350° for 30 minutes.

Restaurant Recipe

Peanut Butter Pie

1 (8-inch) pie crust, baked
1 (8-ounce) package cream cheese, softened
¾ cup peanut butter
1 cup powdered sugar
2 tablespoons milk
1 teaspoon vanilla
1 cup whipping cream

In a large bowl using an electric mixer, blend cream cheese, peanut butter, sugar, milk, vanilla and whipping cream until smooth. Pour into crust; refrigerate at least 30 minutes before serving.

Restaurant Recipe

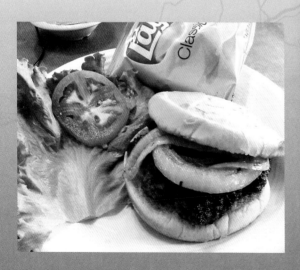

Sheila's Place

915 South Marshall Street
Marshfield, MO 65706
417-859-5647
Find us on Facebook

Sheila's Place, an award-winning restaurant, was voted Best Pan Fried Chicken and Best Desserts in *Rural Missouri Magazine* and Best Restaurant five years running by voters in the *Marshfield Mail*. Sheila's Place, a family-style restaurant, has been a staple in Webster County for more than 22 years. From the gooseberry cobblers, coconut cream pies, pan fried chicken, and fresh cut steaks, Sheila's Place is sure to please all appetites.

Monday–Saturday: 7:00 am to 8:30 pm
Sunday: 7:30 am to 3:00 pm

Coconut Cream Pie

2½ cups milk, divided
¾ cup sugar
4 large eggs, separated
3 tablespoons cornstarch
1 tablespoon butter
1 teaspoon coconut extract
1 cup coconut flakes
1 pie shell, baked

In a saucepan, heat 2 cups milk over low heat. In a bowl, thoroughly whisk ½ cup sugar, ½ cup milk, egg yolks and cornstarch; add to hot milk, whisking quickly to combine. Cook until mixture begins to thicken; cook another 2 to 3 minutes. Remove from heat; add butter, extract and coconut. Stir well; pour into pie shell.

Meringue:

4 egg whites, room temperature
1 tablespoon meringue powder
3 tablespoons sugar
Coconut flakes for top

In a chilled mixing bowl, start whipping egg whites on high speed; add meringue powder then slowly add sugar. Whip until stiff peaks form. Spoon Meringue over pie, sealing edges. Sprinkle coconut on top: bake at 350° for 20 to 25 minutes or until golden brown.

Restaurant Recipe

Pea Salad

4 cups frozen peas
1 cup cubed white American cheese
6 eggs, boiled and chopped
½ cup mayonnaise
½ cup sour cream
1 tablespoon sugar
1 teaspoon salt

In a bowl, mix peas, cheese and eggs together. In a smaller bowl, combine mayonnaise, sour cream, sugar and salt; pour over pea mixture stirring together. Serve.

Restaurant Recipe

Bayou Lunchbox

864 East Highway 60
Monett, MO 65708
417-235-7800
Find us on Facebook

From po'boys and muffulettas to jambalaya and crawfish boils on Saturday, Bayou Lunchbox is sure to please every appetite. They also have a wide variety of vegetarian items to satisfy that healthy soul. Want to sit back, relax, and maybe laugh a little too loud? Just ask to be seated in the banquet room. You will still be served by the attentive, friendly staff. They are spot-on to serve you and keep the good food coming. Don't forget desserts like Southern Comfort custard pie and New Orleans bread pudding.. You just may get to meet Darren Indovina, owner/chef, in person. He likes to visit his guests and make sure you are satisfied.

Monday–Thursday: 11:00 am to 8:00 pm
Friday & Saturday: 11:00 am to 9:00 pm

Shrimp Étouffée

1 stick butter or margarine

1 large onion, chopped

½ cup chopped celery

2 cloves garlic, minced

1 small bell pepper, chopped

1 hot pepper (or several
drops of Tabasco sauce)

2 tablespoons flour

1 pound peeled shrimp (or crawfish
tails or chopped boneless chicken)

Salt and pepper to taste

1 cup water or shrimp stock

¼ cup chopped parsley

Cooked rice

Melt butter in heavy pan; sauté onion, celery, garlic, bell pepper and hot pepper until soft. Add flour, stirring constantly until golden brown. Add shrimp, salt and pepper. Add water or shrimp stock; bring to a boil. Lower temperature; simmer 10 minutes. Add parsley; simmer 5 minutes more. Serve over rice.

Restaurant Recipe

Creole Coffee Ice Cream Punch

6 eggs

½ cup sugar

3 cups CDM Coffee & Chicory,
strongly brewed and cooled

¼ cup bourbon

1 pint vanilla or coffee ice cream

In a large bowl, beat eggs at high speed until slightly thickened. Gradually add sugar, beating until smooth and quite thick. Add coffee and bourbon; mix thoroughly. Pour into a punch bowl or pitcher. Spoon in ice cream; stir well. Allow ice cream to melt slightly to flavor the punch; serve immediately. Makes about 14 servings.

Restaurant Recipe

Red Barn Café and Hen House Bakery

107 West Mount Vernon Boulevard
Mt. Vernon, MO 65712
417-466-4650
Find us on Facebook

If you like chicken-fried steak, catfish, and chicken livers as well as unique items like a chipotle burger made fresh to order, then Red Barn Café and Hen House Bakery is the place for you. The owner, Shari Copenhaver, has been in the restaurant business for 42 years, so she knows how to do it and do it right. Starting as a baker at age 15, she makes the best cakes, pies, and desserts and knows how to satisfy her customer's sweet tooth. Everything is made from scratch. From the breakfast buffet every morning to the Sunday lunch buffet, you will enjoy the finest food anywhere.

Monday–Saturday: 6:00 am to 9:00 pm
Sunday: 7:00 am to 3:00 pm

Frosting for German Chocolate Cake

16 (14-ounce) cans condensed milk

2 pounds butter

48 egg yolks, beaten

4 tablespoons vanilla

8 cups shredded coconut

8 cups chopped pecans

In a double boiler, add condensed milk, butter, yolks and vanilla. Cook until combined well. Remove from heat; add coconut and pecans.

Restaurant Recipe

Shari's Chocolate Cake

12 cups sugar

10½ cups all-purpose flour

4½ cups cocoa

3 tablespoons baking powder

3 tablespoons baking soda

2 tablespoons salt

12 eggs

6 cups milk

4 tablespoons vanilla

3 cups oil

6 cups boiling water

In a large bowl, combine all dry ingredients. Add eggs, milk, vanilla and oil; mix on low speed 2 minutes. Turn mixer to medium speed; mix 5 minutes. Turn mixer back to low speed; add boiling water. Batter will be very thin. Pour batter into sprayed and lined 9-inch round pans. Bake at 325° for 15 to 20 minutes.

Restaurant Recipe

Cheesecake

30 (8-ounce) packages
cream cheese, softened

8 cups sugar

24 eggs

2 tablespoons almond extract

½ cup cornstarch

In a large bowl, cream together cream cheese and sugar. Slowly add eggs and extract beating to mix well. Add cornstarch; mix well. Pour into springform pans. Bake at 225° for 1¾ hours.

Restaurant Recipe

WHAT'S A BUSHWHACKER? GET THE ANSWER HERE

The Bushwhacker Museum, Nevada

From prehistoric tools and fossils to antique medical instruments, women's wedding finery, an old jail, and a child-sized classroom, the Bushwhacker Museum in Nevada (Nevada, Missouri, that is) offers something for people of all ages.

Bushwhacker Museum features more than 10,000 square feet of exhibit space catering to a wide range of interests—Native American exhibits, Civil War artifacts, antique carriages, old handmade quilts, children's toys, antique sidesaddles, and early fire department memorabilia. Learn why the Osage Indian tribe welcomed the first white settlers and why the tribe eventually left the region. Discover why Federal troops during the Civil War called Nevada the Bushwhacker Capital. Find out how the community survived and thrived.

The Bushwhacker Jail is a rare example of prison facilities from the late nineteenth century. It is the oldest structure in Nevada, and one of the few buildings spared when Federal Militia burned Nevada to the ground in 1863. This building functioned as a jail from 1860 until 1960. It was restored for use as a museum in 1965, and entered on the National Register of Historic Places in 1977. You can tour the beautifully restored jailer's family quarters, step inside a grim, dark jail cell, or marvel at the graffiti in the old drunk tank.

The jail cells are a sobering reminder of times when even basic comforts could not be taken for granted, and the keyword for prisoners was containment, not rehabilitation. The only heat for the cell block was from a pot-bellied stove, and the shadows were hardly kept at bay by the single light bulb hanging in the center of the room. The jail was freezing cold in the winter and probably equally uncomfortable in the heat of summer. Not surprisingly, escape attempts were numerous. Some say the old jail is haunted, but you can draw your own conclusions as you tour the iron cell block, and view the yard where Nevada's last hanging took place.

The old jail building housed not just those residents of the cell block but also the jailer and his family. The jailer was generally the sheriff, but sometimes a deputy was given this assignment. It may have depended in part on whether the sheriff was married, since an experienced cook, usually a woman, was needed to prepare meals for the jail residents. The family living quarters consisted of an office, dining room, parlor, and two bedrooms upstairs. These rooms have been restored and furnished in a style correct for the period from 1870 to 1900.

The Museum's building was originally constructed in 1920 as a Ford agency and garage. Today, the Finis M. Moss building houses the Nevada Public Library as well as the Bushwhacker Museum.

Bushwacker Museum
212 West Walnut Street
Nevada, MO 64772
417-667-9602
www.bushwhacker.org
bushwhackerjail@sbcglobal.net

White Grill

200 North Commercial
Nevada, MO 64772
417-667-9388
Find us on Facebook

The White Grill, a little unassuming diner tucked away on the east end of Nevada, opened in 1938. What the little diner lacks in size, it more than makes up for in reputation. The Grill is known for its legendary hand-cut Suzie-Q's (fries), the intimidating but delicious breakfast "mess," and mouthwatering burgers. Over the years, it has seen its share of famous folks and received an endorsement from former President Harry S. Truman that it was "the best damn burger" he ever had. Don't take his word for it, though. Come on by yourself and taste the magic.

Monday–Thursday: 6:00 am to 8:00 pm
Friday & Saturday: 6:00 am to 9:00 pm
Sunday: 7:00 am to 8:00 pm

The Mess

2 tablespoons butter or oil

4 cups peeled diced potatoes

½ cup chopped onion

1 cup chopped cooked ham (bacon or sausage)

2 medium eggs

4 slices American cheese

In a large skillet, heat butter over high heat. Add potatoes and onion; cook 5 to 7 minutes or until lightly browned, stirring often. Stir in ham. Break eggs over the mess; stir to combine. Cook 2 to 3 minutes; when eggs begin to firm, cover with cheese. Reduce heat to medium; cover with lid. Cook 2 minutes or until cheese is melted. Serve immediately.

Restaurant Recipe

Uncle Roosters

29 Enterprise Drive
Seymour, MO 65746
417-935-4120
www.uncleroosters.com
Find us on Facebook

Uncle Roosters is a "fast casual" style restaurant featuring menu items not found in the normal restaurant, such as Chicago hot dogs right from Chicago, Italian beef, homemade barbeque, award-winning chili, and baked beans. In addition, they offer great fried chicken made-to-order, catfish, cod, and shrimp dinners. Don't forget the hand-dipped sundaes and shakes to go with Aunt Bobbi's tasty desserts. The atmosphere is very comfortable and unique. While you are waiting for your food, you can browse the local-made crafts for sale and sign your name on the floor. Uncle Roosters is located on four lane Highway 60 with plenty of parking for trucks, trailers, or RVs.

Monday–Thursday: 10:00 am to 7:00 pm
Friday & Saturday: 10:00 am to 8:00 pm
Sunday: 11:00 am to 2:00 pm

Raw Apple Cake

4 cups finely chopped apples
(red and gold delicious)
2 cups sugar
1 cup butter-flavored Crisco
2 eggs
3 cups all-purpose flour
2 teaspoons baking soda
¾ teaspoon salt
2 teaspoons cinnamon
1 cup coffee
2 teaspoons vanilla
½ teaspoon black walnut flavoring

Topping:

⅔ cup brown sugar
½ cup chopped walnuts or pecans

Put apples into greased and floured 9x13-inch pan. Cream sugar and shortening; add eggs. Sift together flour, soda, salt and cinnamon; set aside. Add flour mixture alternately with coffee to creamed mixture; mix well. Add vanilla and flavoring; mix. Pour batter over apples. Mix brown sugar with nuts; sprinkle over top. Bake at 375° for 40 to 50 minutes.

Family Favorite

Coconut Cake

½ cup shortening

½ cup butter

2 cups sugar, divided

3 cups sifted all-purpose flour

4 teaspoons baking powder

½ teaspoon salt

1⅓ cups coconut milk

1 teaspoon vanilla

1 teaspoon almond extract

⅓ cup shredded coconut

5 egg whites

Cream shortening, butter and 1⅓ cups sugar. Mix flour, baking powder and salt; set aside. With mixer running, add flour mixture to creamed mixture alternately with coconut milk. Add vanilla, almond extract and coconut; mix. Beat egg whites to soft peaks, gradually adding ⅔ cup sugar to make meringue. Fold meringue into batter, just enough to incorporate. Spoon into 2 (9-inch) cake pans sprayed with baking spray. Bake at 350° for 25 to 35 minutes; cake should spring back when touched. Cool thoroughly before frosting.

Frosting:

1 stick butter, softened

1 (8-ounce) package cream cheese, softened

1 teaspoon vanilla

Powdered sugar to taste

2 cups shredded coconut

Cream butter, cream cheese and vanilla. Start adding powdered sugar, 1 cup at a time to desired sweetness. Frost cake; sprinkle with coconut.

Family Favorite

Gailey's Breakfast Café

220 East Walnut Street
Springfield, MO 65806
417-866-5500
facebook.com/gaileysbreakfastcafé

Gailey's Breakfast Café offers a wide selection of breakfast and brunch favorites. This quaint little café was refurbished from an old drugstore that was established in 1942, so when you come to eat, you are also getting a bit of history. If you choose to dine-in or take-out, the caring staff and talented chefs are dedicated to making your dining adventure fun, relaxing, and pleasurable. Whether you bring your family in for quality time together, gather with your friends for brunch and breakfast cocktails, or just want a cup of hot coffee, Gailey's is the perfect place for you.

Sunday–Thursday: 7:00 am to 2:00 pm
Friday & Saturday: 7:00 am to 10:00 pm

Caramelized Bananas with Peanut Butter on Sweet Potato Toast

2 bananas, sliced

½ cup brown sugar

1 teaspoon cinnamon

1 sweet potato, sliced ¾-inch thick lengthwise

½ cup peanut butter

Chocolate chips or walnuts, to top

In a bowl, combine bananas with sugar and cinnamon. In a skillet over medium heat, caramelize bananas. Place sweet potato slices in toaster; keep toasting until done. Microwave peanut butter for 30 seconds or until soft. Place sweet potato "toast" on plate; top with bananas. Pour on peanut butter; top with chocolate chips or walnuts.

**Chef Nick Hanna
Restaurant Recipe**

Sausage Biscuit

Have a family member who's always on the go? This simple setup lets you prepare up to four days in advance so you know you have breakfast covered.

4 baked biscuits

4 small hash browns, cooked

4 baked sausage patties

4 slices Cheddar cheese

Open biscuits; Add hash brown, and sausage; top with cheese slice. Wrap in wax or parchment paper; and tape with masking tape. Place in refrigerator. Now all you have to do is grab one and microwave 1 minute for breakfast on the go. This is best done the day or night before while cooking dinner.

**Chef Nick Hanna
Family favorite**

AMERICA'S ONLY RIDE-THRU CAVE
Fantastic Caverns, Springfield

What's better than a fun and interesting cave tour where the temperature remains a constant and comfortable 60 degrees? The same where you don't have to watch your footing as you tramp through the tour. Fantastic Caverns is a classic tourist attraction offering America's only ride-thru cave for your viewing comfort.

John Knox originally discovered the cave entrance in 1862, but was concerned about the cave being exploited by Union or Confederate governments as a possible source of saltpeter so he kept it quiet until 1867. At that time, he advertised for explorers to help him figure out what he had under his property. A team of twelve women with the Springfield Woman's Athletic Club showed up with torches, lanterns, ropes, and ladders to explore the cave. After the preliminary expedition by the cave gals, who found untouched chambers with large, pristine formations, the owner knew he had something people would pay money to see.

With more than 5,000 caves in the state of Missouri, Fantastic Caverns needed something a little different to help draw visitors. In 1961, the ride-through tours began using post-WWII jeeps with gas-powered engines. The tours were popular, but cave walls don't fare well against car exhaust, so eventually "America's Ride-Thru Cave" upgraded the jeeps to run on cleaner propane.

As the jeep tram travels to the cave entrance, you will see an old steam engine that powered the cave lights in the early days. Once inside, the tour is a mixture of subterranean sightseeing and historical anecdotes. The colorful history includes a period of ownership by the Ku Klux Klan, and there are plenty of factoids about bats and blind cave fish. If you are a cave tour regular, then you won't be disappointed (or surprised) by the requisite moment of darkness when the lights are turned off to show just how dark real dark can be.

If riding through the cave doesn't spoil you enough, you will be glad to know the cave is a constant 60 degrees year-round, and stage lighting accentuates the rock around you, making everything very easy to see.

Fantastic Caverns
4872 North Farm Road 125
Springfield, MO 65803
417-833-2010
www.fantasticcaverns.com

FUN FACTS:

- The cave was renamed "Fantastic Caverns" in the 1950's.

- The cave hosts over 100,000 visitors a year.

- The caverns were used as a speakeasy during the Prohibition years and hosted music concerts during the 1950's and 1960's.

- It's the sole ride-through cave in the United States, and one of only four in the world. The others are in Barbados, France, and Yugoslavia.

Guest Check

SERVER TABLE GUESTS CHECK NUMBER
669806

TAX

TOTAL

189

Crumpie's 11-Point Smokehouse

RR 73 Box 1778, Highway 142
Billmore, MO 65690
417-938-4771

Crumpie's is located in southeastern Missouri on Highway 142 near the 11 Point River and Mark Twain National Forest. This middle-of-nowhere location is popular with locals and motorcycle and car clubs for the perfect "cruise to" with generous helpings. Crumpie's offers barbecue–smoked daily with three kinds of wood–plus made-from-scratch sides, hand-cut steaks, and specialty burgers. Draft beer and wine are available daily. This family-run spot has been open since July 2012, and quickly grew from a husband, wife, and good friend running the whole show.

Wednesday–Saturday: 11:00 am to 8:00 pm
Sunday: 11:00 am to 4:00 pm

Uncle Joe's Potato Salad

10 medium potatoes,
peeled, diced small

1 cup diced onion

1 cup diced celery

¼ cup dill relish

¾ cup sweet relish

1 cup mayonnaise

¼ cup mustard

Salt and pepper to taste

3 boiled eggs, chopped (optional)

Bring potatoes to a boil in a large stockpot with water to cover; cook until potatoes are tender but not falling apart, about 5 minutes. Drain; rinse in cold water. In a large bowl, mix onion, celery, relishes, mayonnaise, mustard, salt and pepper. Add cooked potatoes and eggs, mix well and serve.

Restaurant Recipe

Dew Drop Inn

710 U.S. Highway 61
Bloomsdale, MO 63627
573-483-9992
www.facebook.com/dewdropbloomsdalemo/

The more than 118-year-old Dew Drop Inn is a historical building that has been a lot of things through the years, but today it is a great bar and grill. It has a grand silo on one side of it to pay homage to the facility's days as a flour mill. On each side of the original door was a place where, in the elder days, you checked your guns in before heading to the bar. Now the drop ceilings have been removed, and it is opened up to the tall ceiling and decked out with barn wood and stainless steel. At Dew Drop Inn, you will get good food and a history lesson to boot.

Monday–Thursday: 11:00 am to 10:00 pm
Friday & Saturday: 11:00 am to 1:00 am
Sunday: 11:00 am to 9:00 pm

BBQ Pork Nachos

Fried white corn chips

Dew BBQ Rub

Nacho cheese sauce

6 ounces pulled pork

Dew BBQ Sauce

Banana peppers, chopped

Jalapeños, chopped

Red peppers, chopped

Fry tortilla chips for 3 minutes in deep fryer. Drain; sprinkle with rub. Place 1 serving size on plate; cover with cheese sauce. Add pulled pork on top; cover in barbecue sauce. Place banana peppers on top with jalapeños and red peppers around side. Sprinkle more rub on top.

Restaurant Recipe

Bronco Buster Pizza

⅔ cup Dew BBQ Sauce

1 (12-inch) thin pizza crust

½ cup shredded Gouda cheese

1½ cups shredded cheese blend, divided

¼ cup chopped red onion, caramelized

½ cup Dew pulled pork

½ cup Dew brisket

Dew BBQ Rub

Preheat pizza oven to 500°. Spread barbecue sauce on crust; spread Gouda cheese and 1 cup cheese blend over sauce. Add onion, pork and brisket. Spread ½ cup cheese blend over top: sprinkle rub over top of cheese. Bake 5 minutes, or until crisp.

Restaurant Recipe

Kozy Kitchen

710 US Highway 61
Bloomsdale, MO 63627
573-483-2898
www.facebook.com/kozykitchenIII/

The Kozy, a newly remodeled, family-owned restaurant has a new home behind the Dew Drop Inn. The Kozy was owned by the family and located down the street, the family bought the Dew Drop in 2015, and combined the two restaurants. Each has its own entrance only being separated by the kitchen. The entrance, located on the side of the Dew Drop, will bring you into a new and unique style of barn wood and stainless steel. The Kozy caters for many events and can be reserved for parties. It gives off a real "kozy" environment.

Sunday–Thursday: 6:00 am to 2:00 pm
Friday & Saturday: 6:00 am to 8:00 pm

Spinach Bacon Quiche

1 tablespoon butter

½ cup diced mushrooms

2 teaspoons minced garlic

1 cup bacon pieces

2 cups leaf spinach

⅓ cup shredded Cheddar cheese

⅓ cup Swiss cheese

¼ cup crumbled feta cheese

5 eggs, beaten

1 pint heavy cream

1 unbaked pie shell

Melt butter in a saucepan; add mushrooms, garlic and bacon pieces, cooking until tender. Add spinach; cook until wilted. Add cheeses; mix. In a separate bowl, mix eggs and heavy cream. Cover bottom of pie shell with egg mixture, saving remainder to pour over top. Pour spinach mixture over egg mixture; top with remaining egg mixture. Bake at 350° for 40 minutes.

Restaurant Recipe

Pork Chop Glaze

1 cup pineapple juice

⅓ cup water plus 3 tablespoons, divided

3 tablespoons vinegar

1 tablespoon teriyaki sauce

½ cup brown sugar

3 tablespoons cornstarch

Mix together pineapple juice, ⅓ cup water, vinegar and teriyaki sauce in a pan; heat on stove, stirring constantly. While stirring, add brown sugar. Thicken with cornstarch mixed with 3 tablespoons water. Remove from heat when thick. Enjoy with your preference of cooked pork chops.

Restaurant Recipe

BILLION GALLON LAKE
Bonne Terre Mine, Bonne Terre

Do you love to scuba dive? Have you ever been diving in an underground lake? Bonne Terre Mine is where you can "Dive to the Center of the Earth." It is a national historic site and the world's largest freshwater dive resort, featuring a seemingly endless underground world, frozen in time.

The mine is a giant hole underneath the town of Bonne Terre, hacked out of solid rock over 101 years ago by the St. Joseph Lead Company. Back in the day, the mine's deepest reaches were not underwater. In 1962, the mine shut down and turned off the pumps, and groundwater began pouring in. These days, mine owners Doug and Catherine maintain a constant water level, providing divers with access to their unique underwater vision with water as clear as a swimming pool.

Water conditions remain constant with a more than 100-foot visibility. And there is so much to see from when the place was a functioning mine: shovels, drills, ladders, ore carts, scaffolding, staircases, pillars, slurry pipes, the famed elevator shaft, and much more. The underwater ghost town features pillars, shafts, archways, and walls and ceilings that stretch for miles in all directions. It's a sprawling maze lit with 500,000 watts of high-powered stadium lighting resulting in electric-blue water.

There are lots of planned trails numbered sequentially, and every group of divers is assigned a guide and a safety diver. The dives become more advanced with additional swim-throughs and archways to navigate as the numbers get larger.

Bonne Terre Mine is without a doubt one of the most unusual, beautiful, and relaxing full-service dive resorts anywhere.

Bonne Terre Mine
185 Park Avenue
Bonne Terre, MO 63628
888-843-3483
www.bonneterremine.com

FUN FACTS:

- Bonne Terre is one of the world's largest man-made caverns. Founded in 1860 as one of history's earliest deep-earth lead mines and the world's largest producer of lead ore, it was closed in 1962.

- The mine is a constant 65 degrees year-round; it is never affected by the weather.

Traveler's Table

126 Dillard Mill Road
Davisville, MO 65456
573-244-5300
www.thetravelerstable.com

There is an adage in the restaurant business: location, location, location. We often refer to the Traveler's Table as "the accidental restaurant in the middle of nowhere." There is a story of how we ended up starting a restaurant a mile down a gravel road in the hamlet of Dillard—it is too long to tell here, but if you ask us, we will tell you the whole thing! Besides burgers, steaks, and pulled pork, we bring the cuisines of California and the world down this country road. (Please check our website, since our menu changes daily.)

Open Memorial Day weekend through the second
Saturday in September.
Friday & Saturday: 11:00 am to 8:00 pm
Sunday: 11:00 am to 6:00 pm

The Cuban Sandwich

This is one of the things that "put us on the map." When my dad lived in Florida, this showed up on a number of menus where we ate. I wanted to make it both authentic and just a notch better than the ones I tried.

Cuban Pork:

5 pounds pork butt

Salt and pepper to taste

1 onion, sliced

4 garlic cloves, peeled, sliced into 8 pieces

2 limes, juiced

2 oranges, juiced

1 heaping tablespoon frozen orange juice concentrate

1 scant teaspoon ground cumin

1 tablespoon chopped fresh oregano, or heaping teaspoon dry oregano

2 bay leaves

Sprinkle pork butt with salt and pepper. In a large hot pan over high heat, sear butt fat-side down; turn to sear other side. Remove butt. Turn heat to medium; add sliced onion and brown lightly. Add garlic and lower heat; cook slowly, being careful not to burn garlic. Add lime and orange juices and frozen orange juice concentrate to deglaze pan. Add to slow cooker, getting as much of everything from pan as possible using a spatula. Sprinkle meat with cumin; add to slow cooker. Add oregano and bay leaves. Turn roast in slow cooker with tongs to coat with flavorings. Replace lid; cook an hour on high. Turn to low and cook 8 hours. After it is tender, remove as much fat as possible with a fork and tongs.

Cuban Sandwich:

Soft, wide French bread

Cuban Pork

Yellow mustard

Dill pickle slices (the long sandwich slices are great for this)

Sliced Swiss cheese

6 slices Virginia ham, or other nice deli ham

2 tablespoons butter, melted

1 tablespoon oil

Slice bread lengthwise and pull out some of the inside (discard). Spread bottom slice with a generous amount of Cuban Pork. Squeeze a few good zig-zags of yellow mustard onto the top bread. Place a number of pickles on mustard; top with slices of Swiss cheese to cover. Layer ham over pork. Mix butter and oil together. Put sandwich top on carefully; brush top with butter and oil mixture. Toast sandwich in heated sandwich press until golden crispy and cheese is melted.

Restaurant Recipe

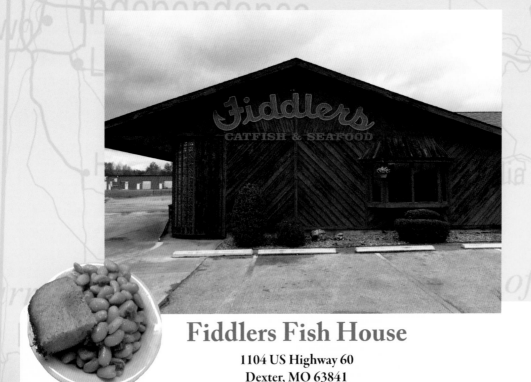

Fiddlers Fish House

1104 US Highway 60
Dexter, MO 63841
573-624-3710

Fiddlers Fish House was established in 1983 by Rick and Marilyn Taylor Williams. Marilyn, being raised on her family's fish farm, was no stranger to inviting crowds over for catfish and hushpuppies. Feeding more than 450 guests on opening day was amazing and it let them know this is what they needed to do. Roy Williams and Toni Culver, co-owners and managers, continue that same family tradition and expanded the menu to include banquets, caterings, and the finest in home-style lunch buffet served daily and on weekends. Today they still share the same great pond-to-plate southern experience to be enjoyed every day.

Tuesday–Thursday: 11:00 am to 8:00 pm
Friday & Saturday: 11:00 am to 9:00 pm
Sunday: 11:00 am to 4:00 pm

Layla & Toni

Vinegar Slaw

12 cups sugar

4 tablespoons celery seed

3 tablespoons yellow mustard

6 cups white vinegar

2 cups water

18 quarts ground cabbage

6 tablespoons salt

6 bell peppers, chopped

1 carrot, grated

In a large pot, add sugar, celery seed, mustard, vinegar and water; bring to a boil. Take off heat; set aside. In a large container, add cabbage, salt, peppers and carrot. Pour vinegar mixture over cabbage mixture; stir well. Let sit 10 minutes. Ready to serve.

Restaurant Recipe

Coconut Cream Pie

⅔ cup sugar

¼ cup cornstarch

Pinch salt

2 cups milk

6 eggs, separated

2 teaspoons vanilla

2 tablespoons butter, melted

2 cups flaked coconut

1 pie crust, baked

In a saucepan over medium heat, mix sugar, cornstarch, salt and milk, stirring constantly until thickened. Add egg yolks, stirring constantly. Remove from heat; add vanilla, butter and coconut. Mix well; pour into pie shell. Top with Meringue.

Meringue:

6 egg whites

½ cup sugar

1 teaspoon vanilla

¼ cup flaked coconut

Beat egg whites until stiff peaks appear; gradually beat in sugar and vanilla. Spread on top of pie, spreading to the edges. Sprinkle with coconut. Bake in preheated 350° oven until golden brown.

Restaurant Recipe

The Depot Cafe

406 Villar Street
Fredericktown, MO 63645
573-561-1333
www.thedepotcafémo.com

The Depot Cafe, located in the historic train depot built in 1917, opened February 2016. Serving both lunch and dinner, enjoy an eclectic collection of freshly prepared foods. From old standards, such as a Rueben sandwich, to something off the beaten path like our Cajun meatloaf sandwich with andouille sausage gravy, there is plenty to choose from. The dinner menu features steaks, seafood, and a few unique items. Daily specials include liver and onions, baked lasagna, seafood gumbo, and chicken pot pie. House made soups and fresh salads are always available, as well as a variety of ever-changing desserts. All desserts are made in house from scratch, including carrot cake, triple chocolate cheesecake, and raisin walnut pie. Service is impeccable and friendly.

Tuesday–Thursday: 11:00 am to 8:00 pm
Friday & Saturday: 11:00 am to 9:00 pm
Sunday: 11:00 am to 3:00 pm

Creamed Potato Soup

¼ pound bacon, diced

1 cup medium diced onion

½ cup medium diced celery

½ cup medium diced carrots

½ teaspoon Worcestershire sauce

2 teaspoons salt

½ teaspoon black pepper

1 dash Tabasco sauce

2 quarts water

2½ pounds red potatoes,
skin on and cubed

½ cup sour cream

¼ cup shredded Cheddar cheese

In large saucepan, sauté bacon until almost crispy. Add onion, celery and carrot. Cooking until tender. Add seasonings, water and potatoes. Bring to a boil; reduce to a simmer. Cook until potatoes are fork-tender. Remove from heat; add sour cream and Cheddar cheese. Using an immersion blender, purée mixture until smooth. Can be garnished with either sour cream or shredded Cheddar cheese and thinly sliced green onions.

Family Recipe

Fire Roasted Tomato Soup

2½ pounds fresh ripe tomatoes

¼ pound fresh green onions

2 ounces fresh parsley, including stems

1 quart milk

1 cup heavy cream

1½ teaspoons chicken base

½ teaspoon black pepper

1 teaspoon salt

1½ ounces tomato paste

Cook tomatoes, green onions and parsley on an inside char broiler or an outside barbecue pit until all vegetables are slightly black. Combine with remaining ingredients in a medium saucepan; bring to a boil. Reduce heat; simmer 15 minutes. Turn off heat. Using an immersion blender, purée until smooth. Strain soup to remove pulp. Return to saucepan; bring back to temperature. Can be served immediately or chilled and served later.

Restaurant Recipe

Wayno's Seafood & Grill

24 Court Square
Fredericktown, MO 63645
573-561-1200
Find us on Facebook

Wayno's Seafood & Grill is the place to go for good food, good friends, and good company. It is exactly the kind of neighborhood joint that makes you feel right at home, where you can expect friendly down-home service with a smile. It's the food, however, that will keep you coming back. From appetizers to the main dish, seafood is the star yet the menu offers plenty for everyone to have something they love—all prepared fresh from the freshest ingredients. Just a few of the favorites are fish, steaks, frog legs, burgers, seafood gumbo, crawfish etouffee, catfish, scallops, soft shell crab, crab cakes, jambalaya, and so much more. Stop by soon and you'll agree, we all love Wayno's.

7 days a week: 11:00 am to 10:30 pm

Red Beans

3 pounds Camellia red beans

3 cups coarse chopped onion

1½ cups coarse chopped celery

¾ cup coarse chopped bell pepper

2 tablespoons minced garlic

1 tablespoon Old Bay seasoning

1 tablespoon Tony's original
creaole seasoning

1 tablespoon chopped parsley

½ tablespoon salt

1 tablespoon Tony's spice
n' herbs seasoning

1 tablespoon Luzianne cajun seasoning

2 pounds Double D sausage,
sliced ⅜-inch thick

1½ pounds ham with skin
& bone (or ham hocks)

Rice, cooked

In a large stockpot, cover beans with 1 gallon water over medium heat. Add remaining ingredients. Cover; simmer 1 to 2 hours, stirring occasionally. Add water as needed. Serve over rice. This makes about 2 gallons.

Restaurant Recipe

Strawberry's BBQ

107 Main Street
Holcomb, MO 63852
573-792-9689
www.strawsbbq.com

WE ARE FAMOUS FOR OUR PORK STEAK!!

Oh my goodness, Strawberry's is the place to go for legendary two-pound pork steaks, cooked to perfection and completely covering your plate. Thanks to World BBQ Grand Champion Pitmaster, Jerry Holsten, this is the place to go for barbecue done right. But, not to be outdone by the pork steak, try the pulled pork, burgers, catfish, and the best sides—like scalloped potatoes and okra—you will ever have the pleasure of eating. This is a little haunt in the middle of nowhere, but don't let the small-town charm fool you. The food is excellent along with friendly, attentive staff.

Monday–Saturday: 11:00 am to 9:00 pm

Slaw

10 cups sugar

5 cups apple cider vinegar

½ cup salt

½ cup celery seed

5 cups canola oil

100 pounds cabbage, shredded

2 (32-ounce) bags diced onions

2 (32-ounce) bags diced
green bell peppers

2 (28-ounce) cans pimentos

In a large stockpot over medium-high heat, melt sugar in vinegar with salt and celery seed; add oil. Continue to cook until mixture comes to a boil; remove from heat and set aside. In a large container, mix cabbage, onions, peppers, and pimentos; pour vinegar mixture over cabbage mixture. Mix well. Ready to serve 200 people.

Restaurant Recipe

BBQ NACHOS WITH JALAPENOS

Strawberry's

Beans

1½ (32-ounce) bags diced onions

1½ (32-ounce) bags diced green bell peppers

1 (10-pound) bag ground pork

3 cups Strawberry's Grand Champion BBQ Seasoning

24 (117-ounce) cans Bush's Baked Beans with sugar and molasses

9 cups Strawberry's Grand Champion BBQ Sauce

In a stockpot, add onions and peppers; cook down. Add pork; brown. Add seasoning: mash with potato masher. Add beans and sauce. Cook over low heat until warmed through. Makes 6 (6-inch) steamer pans. Enough to feed 600 people.

Restaurant Recipe

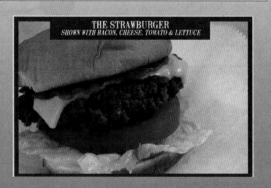

THE STRAWBURGER
SHOWN WITH BACON, CHEESE, TOMATO & LETTUCE

Mom's Chicken and Dressing

1 whole chicken

2 stalks celery, chopped

3 (32-ounce) boxes chicken broth

2 (8.5-ounce) boxes Jiffy Corn Muffin Mix

2 eggs

2⅓ cups milk

1 onion, chopped (or onion flakes)

Salt and pepper to taste

3 tablespoons rubbed sage

Boil chicken and celery in broth until cooked through; set aside to cool. Combine muffin mix with eggs and milk and bake per directions on box for cornbread; cool. Crumble cornbread. Add onion, salt, pepper and sage; mix well. Debone chicken and add meat to cornbread mixture. Strain broth and add to desired consistency. Bake in a large pan at 350° for 1 hour.

Family Favorite

El Carnaval
Mexican Restaurant

2 Locations
127 West Highway 32
Licking, MO 65542
573-674-1221

2250 North Bishop Avenue, Suite B
Rolla, MO 65401
Find us on Facebook

The El Carnaval Mexican Restaurant in Licking has a huge following of patrons that enjoy authentic Mexican foods cooked fresh daily. Come in for a little taste of Mexico from the Angel and Perez families. Enjoy true Mexican cooking by people with more than 20 years experience cooking the best dishes Mexico has to offer. From fish tacos to homemade guacamole, enjoy the true Mexican experience and get a taste of Mexico from the interior, too.

7 days a week 11:00 am to 10:00 pm

Grilled Fish Tacos with Chipotle–Lime Dressing

Marinade:

¼ cup extra virgin olive oil

2 tablespoons white vinegar

2 tablespoons fresh lime juice

2 teaspoons lime zest

1½ teaspoons honey

2 cloves garlic, minced

½ teaspoon cumin

½ teaspoon chili powder

1 teaspoon Old Bay seafood seasoning

½ teaspoon ground black pepper

1 teaspoon hot pepper sauce

1 pound tilapia fillets, cubed

In a bowl, whisk together all ingredients except fillets. Place fillets in a shallow dish; add marinade. Cover; refrigerate 6 hours.

Dressing:

1 (8-ounce) container light sour cream

½ cup chipotle adobo sauce

2 tablespoons fresh lime juice

2 teaspoons lime zest

¼ teaspoon cumin

¼ teaspoon chili powder

½ teaspoon Old Bay seafood seasoning

Salt and pepper, to taste

In a bowl, whisk together all ingredients; refrigerate until needed.

Tacos:

1 (10-ounce) package tortillas

3 ripe tomatoes, seeded and diced

1 bunch cilantro, chopped

1 small head cabbage, cored and shredded

2 limes, cut in wedges

Preheat an outdoor grill for high heat; lightly oil grate. Set grate 4 inches from heat. Remove fish from marinade, draining off any excess; discard marinade. Grill fish pieces 9 minutes, turning once or until easily flaked with a fork. Assemble tacos by placing fish pieces in the center of tortillas with desired amounts of tomatoes, cilantro, and cabbage; drizzle with dressing. To serve, roll up tortillas around fillings; garnish with lime wedges.

Restaurant Recipe

Lambert's Café II

1800 West State Highway J
Ozark, MO 65721
417-581-7655
www.throwedrolls.com

In 1942, with 14 cents in hand, Earl and Agnes Lambert started the family business—Lambert's Café. It has been growing bigger and bigger ever since. The motto—"We hope you come hungry, leave full, and hopefully have a laugh or two."—holds true every day. For more than 70 years, they have entertained visitors with great home-style cooked meals in a roaring atmosphere. On a busy day in 1976, Norman Lambert was handing out rolls in the crowded restaurant. He couldn't reach a patron in the back, so the man yelled, "Just throw the @#*^ thing!" He did. That is how Lambert's Café began throwing rolls.

Monday–Saturday: 10:30 am to 9:00 pm
Sunday: 10:00 am to 9:00 pm

Fried Potatoes & Onions

5 pounds potatoes, sliced ¼-inch thick

1 pound white onions, julienned

¼ cup Lambert's Fried Potato Seasoning

3 cups vegetable (or canola) oil

Place 3 cups oil in large frying pan and heat to 425°. Place a single slice of potato in oil to see if it is hot enough to fry. Add potatoes to oil. Add onions on top. Add seasoning. Cover and cook 5 minutes, without stirring (bottom of potatoes will be brown). Flip and cook another 5 minutes or to your desired "crunch." You're done. Enjoy!

Restaurant Recipe

Norman Ray Lambert's 13 Golden Rules

1. As the Bible says, "Do unto others as you would have them do unto you."

2. "Always offer our guest at least one service they can't receive anywhere else."

3. "You, our guest, are very important, you are the reason we are here! THANK YOU!"

4. "We need you, our guest, much more than we need ourselves."

5. "You, our guest, are always right."

6. "It's our job to take care of you, if we don't someone else will."

7. "If we make a mistake, we will correct it immediately!"

8. "Our simple but powerful rule: Always give you, our guest, more than you expect to get."

9. "You are our guest; guests in our home, not clients or customers, but guests."

10. "Good enough for some is not good enough for us."

11. "The difference between ordinary and extra-ordinary, is: give that little extra."

12. "Quality rather than quantity matters, we offer BOTH."

13. "We do simple things, but in exceptional ways!"

Rob & Kricket's Tater Patch

103 Bridge School Road
Rolla, MO 65401
573 368-3111
www.rollataterpatch.com

Enter the historic Tater Patch in Rolla and you'll experience the comfortable hometown charm of a rustic restaurant and bar featuring exposed wood ceiling beams, a huge stone fireplace, a spacious outdoor deck, along with the best food and nightly entertainment that the Midwest has to offer. Open seven days a week, this fine restaurant offers a full menu featuring smothered taters, pork tenderloin sandwiches, fresh catfish fillets, hand-cut steaks, and prime rib. At night, the Patch comes alive as the area's hottest spot, featuring a full-service bar, pool room, and performances by the area's best regional bands and performers. The Tater Patch has been the area's hot spot for more than 50 years.

Monday–Friday: 11:00 am to 1:30 am
Saturday: 8:00 am to 1:30 am
Sunday: 8:00 am to Midnight

Steak Fajita Tater

1 baking potato

2 teaspoons oil

1 onion, cut in strips

1 green bell pepper, cut in strips

Steak (your choice), cut
into ¼–inch strips

Fajita seasoning, to taste

Butter

Sour cream

Salsa

Preheat oven to 350°. Cook potato for 1 hour or until baked through. In a large skillet over medium-high heat, add oil; sauté onion and pepper until tender. Add steak and seasoning; cook until desired doneness. Remove from heat. Cut potato down the middle lengthwise; squeeze so potato opens wide. Add the sautéed vegetables and steak over the potato and spilling over sides. Garnish with butter, sour cream and salsa.

Restaurant Recipe

UNDERGROUND WINE TASTING PICNIC
Cave Vineyard, Ste. Genevieve

What does a vineyard and cave have in common? Not much unless you are in Ste. Genevieve where you can experience the two together. Cave Vineyard derives its name from the Saltpeter Cave located on the property. Select your wine in the above-ground tasting room located on top of the natural cave wine cellar. Then head down to the cave to sip in subterranean coolness.

The cave, which provides a unique picnic experience, has seating for 100 people. It is an easy, 200-yard walk from the tasting room; shuttles are available on most weekends, summer. and fall. Also, tables are available in our outdoor pavilion, overlooking the vineyard.

Marty and Mary Jo Strussione purchased the Cave Vineyard property in the late 1990's with absolutely no intention of getting into the wine business. While Marty made wine as a young man with his grandfather for personal use, he was really thinking that this piece of southeast Missouri would be the ideal spot to settle into once he retired. Plus, who wouldn't want to own their own cave?

After Marty's retirement, and after building their dream retirement home, Marty decided retirement was not for him and quickly discovered their property was perfect for grape growing. It wasn't long before Cave Vineyard became a family affair. The couple's four daughters, three sons-in-law (affectionately referred to as the SIL's), and nine grandsons all play a role in some aspect of this family business. Whether they are picking grapes, brewing beer, baking biscotti, or working the tasting bar, each has found their niche in the business.

Cave Vineyard is a fun destination with plenty to keep you entertained. Once you've selected your wine of choice, take the homemade trolley down to the cave or take in the scenic views of the vineyard and rolling hills from the pavilion. Bring a picnic basket to enjoy a cool picnic lunch in the cave or let the Cave Vineyard staff pack one for you. There is also a Biscotti Bar in the winery offering up to twelve kinds of biscotti made by the Strussione family using their own family recipe.

Cave Vineyard
21124 Cave Road
Ste. Genevieve, MO 63670
573-543-5284
www.cavevineyard.com

FUN FACTS:

- The 14 acres of grapes at Cave Vineyard are cared for by the Strussione family, who has owned the property since 1995.

- The Missouri Wine and Grape Board, established in 1984, says the wine industry boasts an annual impact of $1.76 billion and includes more than 125 wineries.

- Missouri produces more than 900,000 gallons of wine every year, according to www.visitmo.com.

Café Genevieve

950 Sainte Genevieve Drive
Ste. Genevieve, MO 63670
573-883-9562

Welcome to Café Genevieve, a family restaurant, serving large portions at reasonable prices, where you can swap stories over a meal, a drink or just a cup of coffee, they cut their own steaks, peel the potatoes, and make everything from scratch. This is the kind of comfort food you can't get everywhere. Enjoy week-day lunch specials like meatloaf, chicken-fried steak, catfish, and fried chicken with all the trimmings. The sandwiches are made with just as much concern for taste. Don't forget the desserts with options like cheesecake, bread pudding and German Gooey Butter Cake.

Monday–Friday: 10:30 am to 9:00 pm
Saturday: 8:30 am to 9:00 pm
Sunday: 7:30 am to 6:00 pm

Creamy Coleslaw Dressing

1 cup sugar

3 cups mayonnaise

2 cups Italian dressing

Mix all ingredients until creamy.

Family Favorite

German Gooey Butter Cake

Cake:

1 box yellow cake mix
1 large egg
1 stick butter

In a bowl, combine ingredients; press into bottom of a greased 9x13-inch pan.

Topping:

2 cups powdered sugar
2 eggs, beaten
1 teaspoon vanilla
¼ cup chopped pecans
½ cup shredded coconut

Mix together sugar, eggs and vanilla; mix well. Fold in pecans and coconut; pour over cake. Bake at 350° for 40 minutes.

Family Favorite

Grandma's No-Bake Cookies

The best and fastest cookie ever.

1¼ cups brown sugar
¾ cup white sugar
1 stick butter
½ cup milk
3 cups oatmeal
1 cup shredded coconut
1 teaspoon vanilla
4 tablespoons cocoa

In the top of a double boiler, combine sugars, butter and milk; bring to a boil. Boil 3 minutes, stirring constantly. Remove from heat; add oatmeal, coconut, vanilla and cocoa; mix well. Drop by spoonfuls onto wax paper; let rest until cookies are set. Enjoy.

Family Favorite

Sybill's Saint James

1100 North Jefferson Street
St. James, MO 65559
573-265-4224
www.sybills.com
Find us on Facebook

Sybill's Saint James, set in a beautiful southern plantation-style building in the sweet little town of St. James, treats you to high-quality steaks, seafood, pasta, and other specialties available for both lunch and dinner. They offer seasonal dishes as well as daily and nightly specials. Attention to detail can be seen in everything from the fresh ingredients to the exceptional service. There's also a full bar of local micro brews and specialty cocktails, as well as an extensive but approachable wine list. The gift shop, set in a historic 100-year-old farmhouse, has been transformed into a spectacular shopping experience that offers a selection of unique and affordable home décor and accessories.

Tuesday–Saturday: 11:00 am to 9:00 pm
Sunday: 11:00 am to 3:00 pm
Reservations are always recommended.

Shrimp Cakes with Corn and Avocado Salsa

3 pounds popcorn shrimp, cooked and divided

1 cup panko breadcrumbs

3 tablespoons horseradish

1 cup finely chopped celery

Salt and pepper to taste

1 cup mayonnaise

5 medium eggs

5 tablespoons lemon juice

1 cup finely chopped green onions

Using a food processor, pulse 2 pounds shrimp, 1 pound at a time, 3 to 4 times (do not overprocess). Place processed shrimp and remaining shrimp in a mixing bowl. Add remaining ingredients; mix well. Form into cakes and lightly brown in oil on both sides.

Salsa:

1 cup cut-off corn

¼ cup finely chopped cilantro

2 tablespoons lime juice

¾ cup cubed avocado

3 tablespoons finely chopped red onion

Salt and pepper to taste

Mix all ingredients together. Serve on the side.

Seasonal Restaurant Recipe

Sybill's Signature Salad with Honey Roasted Almond Vinaigrette

Spring mix

Cherry tomatoes

Shelled edamame

Blanched asparagus

¾ cup Hellman's mayonnaise

1 cup honey

¼ cup lemon juice

⅓ cup red wine vinegar

2¼ cups olive oil

Feta crumbles

2¼ cups finely crushed toasted almonds

In a salad bowl, toss together spring mix, tomatoes, edamame and asparagus. In another bowl, whisk together mayonnaise, honey, juice and vinegar. Drizzle in olive oil, while constantly whisking. Toss ingredients in the dressing; top with Feta and toasted almonds.

Restaurant Recipe

A PLACE TO CLEAN UP
Vacuum Museum, St. James

Whether you love to clean, have an itch for fun historical facts, or simply enjoy a quirky adventure, the Vacuum Cleaner Museum is the place to go. You'll find it in St. James, which is located on Historic Route 66 and has less than 4,000 residents.

Travel through time as you learn about the history of vacuum cleaners, starting in the early 1900's, before vacuum motors were even invented. You need lots of muscle if you try to use one of the manually-powered 100-year-old machines.

The vast collection takes you through vacuum history starting in the early 1900s with antiques such as the Royal Model 1 and ending in the present with today's world-class vacuums. Every room is furnished like the era it represents, with World War II paraphernalia in the 1930's/1940's, perfectly pastel décor in the 50's, and shag carpeting and lava lamps in the 70's. Vacuum advertisements from each decade are also displayed throughout the museum to give you a taste of how sales pitches for vacuums have changed over the years. There are even novelty vacuum cleaners such as the Hoover Constellation—a vacuum actually built to float like a hovercraft—and celebrity vacuums used by TV housewives.

You will see more than 600 vacuum cleaners and every one of them in working condition. Much of the collection was generously donated by the museum's curator, Tom Gasko, who obtained a large part of his own collection from legendary organist (and vacuum enthusiast) Stan Kann.

The museum is downstairs from the Tacony Manufacturing Plant where Simplicity and Riccar vacuum cleaners are made. You can even add a short tour of the manufacturing plant to your museum visit. Plan a visit and "Get Sucked into the Fun!"

Vacuum Museum
#3 Industrial Drive
St. James, MO 65559
1.866.444.9004
www.vacuummuseum.com

FUN FACTS:

- Electrolux's 1959 model Automatic F was the first canister vacuum to use a power nozzle.

- The first Clean Air upright was made in 1962, it was Hoover's Dial-A-Matic model 1100.

- During the Great Depression, no vacuum manufacturers went out of business.

The Blue Heron Restaurant

110 Front Street
Van Buren, MO 63965
573-323-8156
www.eatsleepfloat.com

The Landing is located on the banks of the Current River in the foothills of the Missouri Ozarks in Van Buren and is Current River's number one resort destination. Since 1994, The Blue Heron Restaurant at The Landing has been offering exceptional food, personable service, and a great view of the Current River. They proudly feature the creative cooking expertise of Chef Bobby King, who is best known for his four cuts of juicy, charbroiled steaks, including his own eight-ounce, crab-stuffed filet. The full service menu also offers a broad variety of specialty entrées.

Memorial Day to Labor Day: Open 7 nights a week at 5:00 pm until
Off Season: Tuesday–Saturday: 5:00 pm until

Sister's Chicken with a Lemon Butter Wine Sauce

1 bottle Chardonnay

½ stick butter

4 tablespoons chicken bouillon

2 tablespoons dry Italian seasoning

2 teaspoons lemon pepper

2 cups sliced mushrooms

Boneless skinless chicken breasts

Garlic salt to taste

Seasoned salt to taste

Black pepper to taste

Provolone cheese slices

Pour wine in a medium-size saucepan until it boils. After it begins to boil, light it and burn off alcohol. Turn down to a simmer; add butter, bouillon, Italian seasoning, lemon pepper and mushrooms. Simmer 20 minutes; set aside. Heat grill for chicken. Season desired amount of chicken breasts with garlic salt, seasoned salt and black pepper; grill until done. Right before removing the chicken from grill, top with a slice of provolone cheese and melt. Plate chicken; top with wine sauce.

Restaurant Recipe

RESTAURANT INDEX

RECIPE INDEX

S

The Ultimate Venison Cookbook for Deer Camp

Harold Webster once again delights sportsmen with a cookbook that should be on every deer camp shelf. Not only can it be used at Deer Camp, but it also serves as your guide for cooking various venison cuts at home. With just a few ingredients and simple techniques, you can be cooking like a pro.

$21.95 • 288 pages • 7x10 • paperbound • full-color

It's So Easy to Cook Food Your Family will Love

This cookbook series features easy-to-afford, easy-to-prepare recipes your family will love. *Kitchen Memories Cookbook* is a cookbook, memory book, and activity book—all in one—making it so easy to spend time with your family making fun kitchen memories of your own. *Family Favorite Recipes* is a collection of recipes handed down through generations of outstanding cooks that makes it easy to feed your family fast…and deliciously.

EACH: $18.95 • 256 pages • 7x10 • paperbound • full-color

The Ultimate Backyard Barbeque and Tailgaiting Cookbook

Great American Grilling is the ultimate grilling, barbecuing, and tailgating cookbook featuring insider hints, pit-proven tips, and tried-and-true techniques for year-round outdoor cooking.

$21.95 • 288 pages • 7x10 • paperbound • full-color

State Hometown Cookbook Series

A Hometown Taste of America, One State at a Time.

Each state's hometown charm is revealed through local recipes from real hometown cooks along with stories and photos that will take you back to your hometown . . . or take you on a journey to explore other hometowns across the country.

EACH: $18.95 • 240 to 272 pages • 8x9 • paperbound

**Alabama • Georgia • Louisiana • Mississippi
South Carolina • Tennessee • Texas • West Virginia**

Church Suppers
Makes a Great Gift

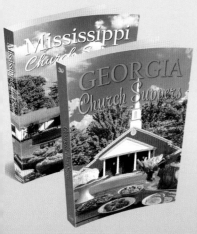

It is available at many of the churches included in this book. If you can't find it locally, call 1-888-854-5954 or visit us online at www.GreatAmericanPublishers.com to order.

Mississippi • **$21.95** • **288 pages** • **7x10** • **paperbound** • **full-color**

Georgia • **$18.95** • **256 pages** • **7x10** • **paperbound** • **full-color**

Eat & Explore Cookbook Series

Discover community celebrations and unique destinations, as they share their favorite recipes.

Experience our United States like never before when you explore the distinct flavor of each state by savoring 250 favorite recipes from the state's best cooks. In addition, the state's favorite events and destinations are profiled throughout the book with fun stories and everything you need to know to plan your family's next road trip.

EACH: $18.95 • 240 to 272 pages • 7x9 • paperbound

**Arkansas • Minnesota • North Carolina
Ohio • Oklahoma • Virginia • Washington**

State Back Road Restaurants Series

From two-lane highways and interstates, to dirt roads and quaint downtowns, every road leads to delicious food when traveling across our United States. The STATE BACK ROAD RESTAURANTS COOKBOOK SERIES serves up a well-researched and charming guide to each state's best back road restaurants. No time to travel? No problem. Each restaurant shares with you their favorite recipes—sometimes their signature dish, sometimes a family favorite, but always delicious.

EACH: $18.95 • 256 pages • 7x9 • paperbound • full-color

Alabama   **Kentucky**   **Missouri**   **Tennessee**   **Texas**

Don't miss out on our upcoming titles—join our Cookbook Club and you'll be notified of each new edition.

www.GreatAmericanPublishers.com • www.facebook.com/GreatAmericanPublishers

---

ORDER FORM

Mail to: Great American Publishers • 501 Avalon Way Suite B • Brandon, MS 39047
Or call us toll-free 1.888.854.5954 to order by check or credit card.

❑ Check Enclosed

Charge to: ❑ Visa ❑ MC ❑ AmEx ❑ Disc

Card#_____

Exp Date _____

Signature_____

Name_____

Addre

City _____ State _____ Zip _____

Phone_____

Email_____

QTY.	TITLE	TOTAL
____	_____	_____
____	_____	_____
____	_____	_____
____	_____	_____
____	_____	_____
____	_____	_____
	Subtotal	_____
	Postage ($4 first book; $1 each additional)	_____
	Order 5 or more books, get FREE shipping	
	Total	_____